DATE DUE

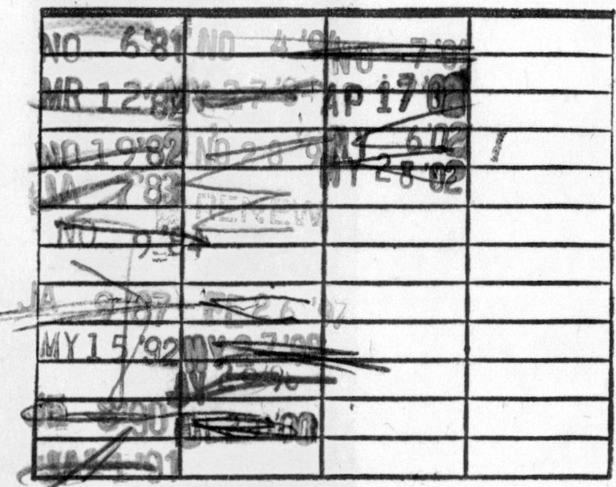

COSTUMES AND SETTINGS FOR STAGING HISTORICAL PLAYS

Volume 4
The Georgian Period

COSTUMES AND SETTINGS FOR STAGING HISTORICAL PLAYS

JACK CASSIN-SCOTT

Volume 4
The Georgian Period

Plays, Inc. *Boston*

First American edition published by Plays, Inc. 1979

Library of Congress Cataloging in Publication Data

Cassin-Scott, Jack.
Costumes and settings for staging historical plays.

CONTENTS: v. 1. The classical period. v. 2 Medieval. v. 3. The Elizabethan and Restoration period. v. 4. The Georgian period.

1. Costume—History. 2. Theaters—Stage-setting and scenery. 3. Historical drama. I. Title.
PN2067.C33 1979 792'.025 78-26037
ISBN 0-8238-0237-X (v. 4)

Printed in Great Britain

CONTENTS

INTRODUCTION

This fourth volume in the Costumes and Settings for Historical Plays Series covers the period from Early Georgian to the French Directoire and First Empire.

This exciting and interesting period of about one hundred years, embodies, for the costume designer, the real thrill and exciting world of historical costume; pulsating with vitality, forming new styles and changing ideas. Never before had such opportunities arisen and fashions of the earlier periods which were thought beautiful, appear, on closer inspection, clumsy, cumbersome and uncomfortable.

Unlike most other art forms, costume and stage design need a great deal of co-operation between designer, craftsman, actor, actress and spectator. It is this combination which gives the designs life and character. Theatre is after all very much a visual form of art.

Within the limitations imposed by the size of this volume, attempts have been made to select from a mass of material, sufficient reference to show the costumes and stage settings of the period. Finer details which do not in themselves clarify the purpose or might even deter from the main silhouette, are omitted.

Stage designing is not in itself the art of meticulous detail so much as a clear general artistic impression. Aspiring designers must always remember that they are presenting settings and costume to a modern and not to a contemporary audience. There must be an immediate comprehension through the design, although dealing with a play by a great dramatist of that period. Designers must therefore harness their imagination to replicate the basic quality of the costumes and stage setting which had made that particular play survive.

A glance back to the beginning of the eighteenth century, the Baroque and Rococo styles, an age of elegance, so well portrayed through the arts and writings of that period, all of which changed so drastically with the revolution in France and which had its repercussions throughout Europe. It was an era of violent contrasts. Fashion changes that had for so long been in subversive undercurrent, now blossomed, pushing aside the earlier conservatism of the century. The tide had turned, and far reaching political developments had a distinct bearing on future costume design in fashion. Freedom and change was the cry of the people, and costume in its new found release reached at times incredible and ridiculous extremes by both sexes. The costume designer, especially, must reflect how these upheavals affected, very strongly, historical costume, which, whilst giving greater freedom, strangely produced a lowering of acceptable behaviour standards of the previous period.

The 'cotton war' which had started in the seventeenth century and spilled over to the eighteenth century presents to the costume designer the task of assimilating the vogue which had caught on throughout Europe, for painted and printed cottons. There was a great demand for this type of material for the more simple garments. The designer, and those interested in costume, should visit the many museums which have dresses and materials in a state of good preservation from this period. The new-found knowledge of colour and dyes made great changes in everyday costume. Towards the end of the century bleaches became a practical proposition with the use of chlorine. These new possibilities increased production and therefore came within the reach of many more people regardless of rank or social standing. Under Louis XIV colouring of materials became brighter, at times reaching almost garish hues. Later the colouring became more subtle and subdued, decoration generally became richer and more ornate, but plain and paler tone were considered more tasteful.

The opportunities for the costume designer for this period are so bountiful with so much information readily available that it is almost difficult to know where to begin. Alongside the research the customs and society should also be studied.

The art of stage historical costume is designed with the innovation of carefully executed exaggeration, and is an essential factor. Larger than life attitude to theatrical costume is most important. The costume must make a strong visual impact to enable the actors to express the characters which they play. The designer must bear in mind the two main influences on costume — the human and the historical. The human influence is represented by the personal habits and the living conditions of the people whether rich or poor to the social standing of persons. The historical is shown by the trends of fashion within the social structure of the period caused by political, industrial, exploration, exploitation and man's inventiveness.

The theatre at this period provided inspiration and aroused great interest to the fashionable ladies of the day, they copied many of the styles which were often a compromise between the previous century and the vogue in fashion: the audiences accepted these without question until about mid-century when historical accuracy became the 'in' thing. Today most audiences delight in seeing actors and actresses dressed in realistic copies of historical costumes against the appropriate background. A certain authenticity has a great impact on the viewing audience. Therefore the designer must have a good eye for detail, although not minute detail, and his design will always be appreciated.

The *stage setting* must be part of the presentation, an interwoven link along with costume and acting, but must always be a significant part of the action of the drama nonetheless. This period offers much to the stage designer from the heavy Baroque grandiose décor to the delicate Rococo, Louis XV and Louis XVI styles. *Stage properties*, so much a part of stage settings, must follow the influences of both the English and French style of decoration and furniture. Museums throughout Europe have a wealth of this contemporary period material and pictorial information. Under the banner of stage properties comes this hardworking department, the weapons and equipment of the soldiers, musical instruments, domestic utensils, jewellery and 'hand and costume' properties.

The illustrations are taken wherever possible from contemporary and impeccable sources, redrawn and simplified, leaving out the finer detail, without I hope, losing the sense of balance of the design and keeping to the essential shape and silhouette. It is impossible to show all the styles of costumes worn. If I have stimulated the would-be designers to further their knowledge on this subject by researching themselves, they will share my genuine love and interest of theatre. It will further their ability in transferring that feeling into a stage picture making the period that is being enacted come to life.

A short chapter stresses the importance of lighting and the designer's need to understand its application.

THE COSTUME

Lady in the full evening dress of the open robe style cut in the high waisted fashion with the elbow length sleeves. Long gloves and a headdress of feathers were worn c 1800

Creating stage costume must never be compared with fashion designing. They are two distinct arts. Fashion is adapting the garment to the person whilst stage costume is fitting the character to the garment. In designing fashion the latest caprices or the *dernier cri* of fashion is most important; the historical stage costume is only concerned with the character and mood of a bygone era. So treat the stage costume with consideration of the character first, then create it with the role the character must play.

Costumes are an integral part of the historical stage picture and are characterized by their structure — in essence their silhouette — thus the exact period to which the costume belongs can easily be recognised. They should be in character with the set design, emphasizing yet harmonizing with the theme of the background, but contrasting enough to stand out.

Research of this particular period is not nearly as difficult as the previous eras outlined in this series. Most museums throughout the world have many fine examples of contemporary costumes. Many art galleries have also a fine pictorial history of the dress of the period. I advise the designer to visit and study these very carefully; an outline of the costume is really all that is required in the first instance. Once the main silhouette has been captured, innovation and adaptability take over. When creating a costume the primary consideration must be 'does the design in any way curtail the action of the character', if it does it must be redesigned. The movement of the body is more important than authenticity of the costume, and the designer's imagination must be brought into full play. Remember also that decoration is important but must not take over from the costume design or structure.

The first production meeting and play-reading is most important, here is where the first ideas are formulated and

Man in double breasted coat with full at the shoulder sleeves. The high collared waistcoat revealed the high stock neckwear. High waisted breeches had fullness on the hips with a closer fitting at the knee. The headwear was the high-fronted bicorne

Lady is dressed in the high waisted, short puffed sleeved muslin costume with a full boa and shawl c 1808 the first rough sketches are made. The choice of roles is also very important, because the designer comes face to face with the characters who are to be costumed, and this is the moment when the designer starts to apply his or her knowledge and know-how.

The *male historical costume* at this early period of the eighteenth century should present no problem for the designer. There was no great change for general wear until the last third of the century. The French influence remained from the late seventeenth century, the tunic and vest was now called a 'coat' and a 'waistcoat'. The coat had become a loose hanging, long waisted, collarless, knee-length garment, worn over a knee-length sleeved waistcoat. The waisted coat had reinforced skirts with large wedge-shaped pleats inserted and stiffened with buckram or whalebone. The effect was a flared coat skirt which had three vents reaching to hip level one on either side and one at the centre back. Over the hips one at each side were low-set large pockets with flaps. The sleeves were straight, with deep, closed, all-round cuffs, which during the period became larger reaching the elbows. The popular fashion, designers please note, was to leave unbuttoned to the waist, both the coat and the waistcoat to reveal a frilled shirt front and cravat which was often loosely tied; shirt cuffs of lace or lawn showed below the coat cuffs.

Breeches were at this time closer fitting than the previous decade and were knee length. Over these were worn long stockings which came up over the knee and were gartered just below the knee. It was common to have a different material for breeches, velvet, camlet, buckskin or frieze. Silk brocade was usually reserved for dress wear. The fashionable Englishmen wore the three pieces of costume made from the same material, which later in the century became the popular mode.

A long loose protective coat with a flat turned-down collar called the 'frac' or 'frock' worn by agricultural workmen and servants, made from ticking, sacking or twill was now accepted by gentlemen of fashion. Now made from a woollen stuff its popularity increased and by the end of the period was called the 'frock coat'.

I have described the basic male costume to show the stage costume designer the subtle changes which took place towards the end of the century. The flared skirt of the coat went completely out of fashion. The leading edges of the coat, to ensure an easier movement for the legs, were cut away from the waist and sloped in a backward direction. Sleeves were lengthened and became closer fitting with much smaller cuffs. The waistcoats became shorter with wide lapels and were buttoned up; the collars were worn high.

The knee-length breeches remained in fashion fitting closer to the thighs, the stockings were no longer worn over the knees but beneath the breeches.

By the end of the century the skirts of the coat were further cut away and were represented only by a short square-cut tail at the back. The short cut-away front became a double breasted version.

The great coat, after about mid-century became the more popular garment and replaced the cloak.

To the costume stage designer the male costume of the eighteenth century would be incomplete without the essential item of fashion, the wig. Working people can often be costumed wearing their own hair, but for the fashionable male, before the end of the century, it would be unthinkable. A study of wigs is very important, they changed throughout the period. Wigs are best hired from a good costumier. They can be made, but with a great deal of difficulty, and then only with patience and clever hands, as it is an art unto itself. The wearing of wigs lasted almost to the end of the century and were constructed from a variety of materials — usually human hair — but these were expensive, so horse or goats' hair was substituted.

Young lady in a ball gown, high waisted with a low décolletage and full skirt, short sleeves were worn with long, over the elbow, gloves c 1805

The three-cornered hat was the most popular hat of the eighteenth century, the round hat was worn by the less fashionable people and workers.

From this basic outline of the male costume the costume designer can face the first production meeting with confidence and will certainly help to come to an early decision on how the character should be dressed. The stage costume designer must now use his or her ability to determine the social status and the character of the individual by the manipulation of the basic costume.

As in all fashion history there are those who break away from the normal mode of the day; this period was no exception. The latter part of the century saw first the *Macaronis*, an Italian innovation, with exaggerated wigs and headwear. After the revolution came the *Incroyables* which, although

Officers and a soldier of 1705 with the collarless coats with buttons from neck to hemline. The officers are wearing heavy sashes around their waists and feathered three-cornered hats

Lady in a Court hooped ball costume, elaborately embroidered with lace and fringing. The decorative headwear had 'nodding' feathers c 1800

confined to France, was a curious mixture of fashionable items and the English country gentleman's clothes. These are described more fully in the main body of the text under their period. These caricatures of historical costume present the costume designer with a delightful problem, as the costume itself leaves much to the talents and imagination of the designer.

Included in the male costume designs must be the various accessories which were worn or carried during the century, these included, watches, fobs, snuff-boxes, muffs and until almost the end of the century swords were carried by gentlemen.

Women's historical costume of the eighteenth century was more affected than that of their male counterpart. This was a time of great liberalism and a great new transformation took place. In the previous periods the men had been more showily dressed than the women, but now not only did the female costume become equal but also soon overtook them in sumptuous splendour.

At the beginning of the century women's costume continued with the rigid and conservative decorum of the previous decade. The high fontange became smaller developing into a 'pinner', a small circular cap worn flat on the crown of the head. For the women's dress the designer of historical costume must take a glance back in history. After the first decade of the eighteenth century when the tight corsage and slit skirt with the bunched up overskirt at the back to give a bustle effect was worn, came the reintroduction of the Elizabethan farthingale. This hooped petticoat, as it was called, developed into many variations and remained in vogue in some form or the other until almost the end of the century, even later as court wear.

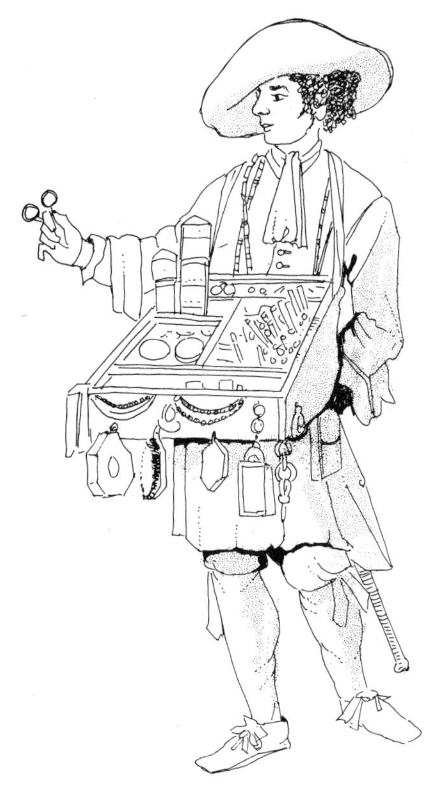

Street trader of 1711, turned up hat and three-quarter length coat

The early part of the century has been labelled as being 'theatrical' in its colour sense, this is possibly true as the materials under Louis XIV were indeed garish. The stage costume designer must go to all lengths to preserve and foster this effect and if possible to emphasize this very trend. The problem for the designer is the following part of the period, up to about 1780, when colours were invariably harmonious, soft, subtle and harsh hues being avoided. From the gay colouring of the early years of the eighteenth century followed a period of tasteful and refined delicacy of colour combinations and patterns. It was a century famous for its brocades, silk weaving, chintzes and painted calico. The French refugees, the Huguenots, brought with them to England the art of silk weaving in 1685 after the revocation of the Edict of Nantes by Louis XIV. They founded the Spitalfields weaving industry and gained for England a large share in the fashionable world.

Again for the stage costume designer in the last twenty years of the century colour became the aggressive answer to the changing world. Splashes of loud brilliant colour were in keeping with the tempo of the times; no longer were the colours in harmony, blending and restful. They became loudly accentuated contrasts vying with one another in their bold coarseness.

The universal trend of white for women's clothes with the inevitable dash of high colour was characteristic, mingling with the contrasting men's costume and military uniforms. Such was the picture of war-torn Europe by the end of the eighteenth and the beginning of the nineteenth centuries. War is at all times a great emotional experience and this showed at this period in the extravagant and ridiculous extremes of costume and colour practised by both men and women.

The epoch of the first Rococo must be its lack of moderation in all things especially in costume. The French Revolution reflected in the costume bringing with it a more practical outlook and an extension of fashion to other sections of the population. The beginning of the nineteenth century saw men's costume grow less colourful, varied and decorative.

Women's costume of the eighteenth century fell into three main classifications: *open robe* in variations, *closed robe*, later known as the round robe, and the *separate bodice and skirt style*. These are explained later in the text. Such names were given as *robe à l'anglaise*, the basic garment of the period; *robe battante*, a loose style of costume; *robe à la française*, the popular sack costume; *polonaise* an open gown with a looped-up overskirt. Many such names will confront the stage designer, most will be included in the main costume section, but the need for more personal research is again strongly recommended.

Hats and hairstyles were worn in great profusion throughout the period. The ever popular mob-cap evolved from being very large to becoming just a brief head covering.

The *Directoire and First Empire* period of the early nineteenth century, brought a more simplified version of women's

Redingote of Napoleon and hat 1815

dress on the classical costume line. The high waisted 'Empire line' becoming the accepted fashion for the whole of Europe.

The study for the costume designer of materials is most essential, with a greater emphasis on the cheaper types of materials. It is the responsibility of the designer to keep a close watch on the costing of this part of the production. These less-expensive materials can, with ingenuity, be transformed, under stage lighting conditions, to represent the original expensive clothes.

I have tried to give a mental and pictorial view of the costumes which were worn by the people of their era and have drawn on contemporary sources in order to give a better idea of how they appeared in those times.

Lady in close fitting, back fastening bodice coming to a point. Gown over a dome shaped hoop, hanging sleeves

Man in coat with shorter waistcoat, turned back lapels. High gaiters c 1734

Admiral's uniform of 1805

Early Georgian

This was indeed an age of violent contrasts. It was the transitional period between the heavy Baroque and the delicate Rococo styles. The period was of great upheaval and change. England had accepted a German as king and France had a Régence, or regency, lasting from 1715 until 1723.

It was during this era of the regency of Philippe of Orléans on behalf of the infant Louis XV, that the formality in dress gave way to a less stiff and pompous way of life, with it a significant alteration in the social structure. The large middle class were, because of the growth of commerce, becoming more affluent and, with this greater influence, began to dictate the style of fashion.

The whole of Europe was at War at sometime or other during this period. Wherever they were fought, these wars affected fashion and costume styles. In the Great Nordic War 1700-1721, Sweden waged war against Denmark, Norway, Poland-Saxony, Prussia and Russia. This war saw the end of the Swedish dominance in the Baltic, bringing Russia very much closer to Europe. During almost the same period, the War of the Spanish Succession 1702-1714 was also being fought. This war involved Austria, England and the Netherlands on the one side and France, Spain, Bavaria, Portugal and Savoy on the other. During this conflict both Portugal and Savoy deserted their own side and joined forces with the enemies of France. The Treaties of Utrecht and Rastadt ended the war but changed the balance of power in Europe. France lost most of her textile trade, the silk and cloth industries were ruined due to the sea blockade by England. After the treaties she gradually regained her former prosperity.

Characteristic of this period was the influence of the Eastern culture. Peter the Great of Russia sought the culture of Paris and London, and in doing so brought about a fashion in fur hats affected by artists and writers. Indian chintz and the solf colours of the Chinese silks were extensively used.

Costume in general became more comfortable and practical to wear, and women's costume especially, abandoned the formality of the late Baroque style. The bustle effect and the long train disappeared and both male and female took on a conical silhouette. Whilst still retaining the symmetry of the Baroque, fashion became gentler and more delicate.

Man in a brocaded suit and morning cap. The lady is wearing the voluminous 'robe battante', a sack dress variation

The most revolutionary change in women's fashionable costume was the reintroduction of the hoop. This had gone out with the abandonment of the Spanish farthingale a hundred years previously.

At first the comfortable contouche, which had formally been the loose fitting housecoat, was supported by a canvas petticoat with metal bands, then changed to a cotton petticoat with a frame of whalebone. The new name of pannier, after the French for a type of basket, was a cage structure made from whalebone, cane or wire, which first appeared in England about 1718 and in Paris the following year. But unlike the farthingale, or the later crinoline, the pannier extended only at the sides. The width became extreme, but such was the fashion that even stair rails were curved to allow free passage on the staircases for these voluminous skirts.

In men's fashion the essential line remained unchanged although the coat and waistcoat became narrow and closer fitting across the shoulders and the coat, worn open, had a greater flare of the skirts. The most remarkable characteristic of men's costume for this period was the wig. The redingcote or riding coat which came to Europe via England in 1725 was to become a fashionable garment, with variations, and worn throughout the century.

This first thirty years of the eighteenth century saw the beginnings of the great changes which lay ahead in fashionable costume. The French fashions were awaited throughout Europe, the pre-eminence and popularity of their gowns left them in complete supremacy, regardless of the British and Eastern competition. The French court mistresses, with their fabulous wardrobes, were the forerunners of the French claim as uncontested leaders of fashion.

Close fitting bodice fastened down the front. Small straw hat c 1710

Women's clothes At the beginning of the eighteenth century, the outer clothes for women were of the popular gown and petticoat variety. The bodice and skirt were often joined together. This was known as the open robe style (although this was not the contemporary term) which displayed the gown open in front revealing the petticoat, which was not, as its name may suggest, an undergarment but was an essential part of the costume. The décolletage was a deep square with a close fitting bodice which was open down the centre bordered with revers, usually double, slightly overlapping, called robings, which came from a band at the nape of the neck and brought forward to meet at waist level. The opening in front between the robings was filled in either by a stomacher, corset or a sleeveless under-bodice, the latter was less popular. The stomacher was usually a decorative V-shaped panel, which was stiffened with pasteboard or busks. The straight upper border formed the low square décolletage. The decoration of the stomacher was either by heavy embroidery or trimmed with 'échelles' of ribbon. Plain stomachers were usually concealed by large neckerchiefs, which encircled the shoulders and bosom, then falling to the waist where it was tied into position by ribbons. The inverted V-shaped opening in the front of the skirt was pulled back and bunched up to give the effect of a 'false rump' or bustle, and to reveal the flounced, embroidered petticoat, which was sometimes partially concealed by an apron. The sleeves of the bodice ended just below the elbow with turned-up cuffs, the sleeve was pleated at the shoulder the join being concealed by the robings, it fitted close to the armhole; then widened towards the elbow. The sleeve was wide to allow the full chemise sleeve and ruffle to come through. After 1720 the bodice had a round décolletage without robings and buttoned down the front to the waistline. The overskirt opening with an inverted V was now joined to the bodice and became the vogue. The sleeves were now straight cut. This type of gown costume was worn with a fontange headdress which became unfashionable in the first decade and the smaller lace cap took over.

Early sack gown Coming into fashion within the first decade was the wide flowing dress of French origin, the sack dress. It was a large shapeless gown, in silhouette not unlike a bell tent. Although frequently called the Watteau Gown it seems to have been in use before the artist's drawings of 1720. It was, however, a simple type of dress being very wide and open down the front with the characteristic of a long wide pleat or fold hanging from the neck down the back. Other innovations of this gown had double or triple pleats stitched down from the neck to the shoulder, then allowed to fall free to the hem. In the front, triple pleats were sewn down at the shoulder seam or held by a loop and button, allowing fullness on either side of the front edges which came to a point at the waist, leaving a space which was covered by a stomacher. The sack gown was usually secured by loops and buttons. Below, the gown was secured by ribbon ties or buttons, or was sewn up, in the latter case the gown was put on over the head. The elbow length sleeves had cuffs which were closed or winged. The fullness of the skirt was sometimes caught up into the side placket holes

Open robe dress with stomacher; sleeves with flounces, crossed neckerchief Small apron. Man with bag-wig. Buttoned round cuff. Stockings over the knees c 1759

Girl in low décolletage dress with round-eared cap with lappets tied under the chin. Man in fashionable costume c 1750

for access to the pockets, which when panniers came into fashion were placed under them, with the name of *robe retroussée dans les poches*. The sack gown enjoyed many variations, the style was particularly popular among the younger ladies and children. The frock, as it was called, for the younger element had the additional variance of the false hanging sleeve; which were long pieces of material attached to the back of the sleeve and allowed to hang down the back on either side. This style lasted until about 1730 when it again changed.

The introduction of *hoops* came in at the end of the first decade of the century. The term 'reintroduction' would perhaps be more to the point as these were merely the rehashing of the Elizabethan farthingale which fell out of fashion a hundred years previously and vanished from the women's costume in France and England. They were, however, still retained by the courts of Spain and Portugal. At first the petticoat was reinforced with hoops of cane or whalebone in preference to the starched petticoat. The hoops quickly developed into various forms of contraptions, from the pannier style to take on funnel shapes, dome shapes, pyramid shapes, pannier à bourrelets, which flared out at the bottom of the gown, elbow pannier, on which the lady could rest her arms or the short padded petticoats lined with horse-hair, often called 'considerations'. From the gum-starched petticoat reinforced with two or three tiers of whalebone and rather short, to the cage designed hoops made from cane, whalebone and wire. Various shapes became fashionable at different times depending on the caprices of the fashion modes of the times.

The stage designer must make careful study of the 'hoop' fashion if he is to be historically correct. The hoop, as already stated, was usually constructed of whalebone, wire, or osier-rods, held in place by ribbons. The first structure resembled the shape of a basket worn on either side, and was called after the French word for basket, *panier*, and is always referred to by that name. The exact origin is a subject of controversy but this calf-length underskirt was reputed to have been worn by actresses to give a narrow waist silhouette. Whatever the origination it assumed its characteristic shape by the third decade of the eighteenth century. The pannier, however, unlike the earlier farthingale, did not distend all the way round, but took on an oval bell shape, extending sideways with a circumference sometimes as wide as 11 or even 18 ft — some 6 metres. The 'cupola coat', or the bell hoop, was dome-shaped and varied in size, the smallest being called a pocket hoop, both were worn almost the whole of the period; but lasting only to about mid-century was the fan hoop which had a pyramidal shape which constricted the front and back into a fan-shaped structure, allowing the skirt to curve up on either side and inclined to tilt with the movement of the wearer. The oblong hoop was an excessive wide-hipped version which lasted into the next period of the eighteenth century. By the 1730s the hoops were covered with strong material such as canvas but often by the wealthier classes were covered in a silk damask, and attached round the waist by draw-strings.

The gown Women's costume in this period may be classified for convenience into three sections, open robe, closed robe and the separate bodice and skirt. The open robe was as its name implies a gown open in the front and worn with a petticoat. The bodice was close-fitting, low décolletage with the edges being decorated with sewn-down flat revers, known as robings. The low cut bodice front was filled in with a V-shaped panel or stomacher, these were often highly decorative and stiffened with padding, busk or pasteboard. The joins of the stomacher, which formed the square décolletage, were hidden by the robings. They were secured either with tabs or were laced from eyelet holes. The closed bodice had a round décolletage and buttoned down the front to the waist being joined to the overskirt to the inverted V opening. The sleeves for both styles were to just below elbow length and finished with a cuff (turned up) or with flounces.

The overskirt was pleated to the bodice with broad pleats which were so placed to point towards the side seam. A typical method of gown construction was the *corsage en fourreau* which was a method of cutting a part of the bodice and skirt in one at the back without a seam line at the waist. There were slight variations according to the type of hoop worn. The overskirt of the open robe had an inverted V-shape opening in the front, which allowed the elaborate embroidered or quilted petticoat to be seen. For court wear the petticoat was often flounced. A variation of the open robe was the popular Mantua. This was fashionable during the first half of the century, made of a rich material, richly embroidered, the bodice was unboned and the overskirt was trained. It was worn for all social occasions, balls, funerals, weddings and court. It was frequently worn with a buckled belt. The closed robe, also known at a later date as the round gown, was a close-fitting bodice and petticoat joined together, frequently with an opening in the front of the skirt. The three variations of the closed robe were, first, the style known as the wrapping gown which was popular from the first decade to half way through the century. It had a round décolletage, a close fitting bodice with no robings and as its name suggests it had a wrap-over front continuous with the skirt, it could be wrapped either over to the left or to the right, tightly or loosely. If loosely wrapped over it was usually secured with a brooch or a ribbon girdle. The low décolletage was filled with lace tucker and a modesty piece. The sleeves were threequarter length very loose fitting and had a turned back cuff from which emerged double or treble ruffles. It was worn with almost any hoop of the period. Secondly and very popular during the 1730s and 40s was the edge-to-edge front closure of bodice gown. The bodice was similar to the wrapping bodice, close fitting, no robings and a low round décolletage. The front had an edge to edge

Servant girls. Left: round eared cap without lappets, basques, petticoat and full apron c 1750
Girl on right in dormeuse cap. Open sack back over-gown. Large apron c 1780

closure with the aid of jewelled clasps or, by the not so wealthy, by ordinary hooks and eyes. The back of the bodice which was close-fitting joined the skirt in the *corsage en fourreau* style. The skirt was made with a front 'fall' which when pleated into a waistband with strings was secured at the back under the bodice, and when gathered together the pleats of the skirt hid the placket slits produced by the fall. The sleeves had narrow cuffs. A modesty piece and a tucker were always worn.

The third variation, the sack, or 'sacque', was worn as a closed robe until about 1740, and not after 1750 by which time it became an open robe. The earlier style from the first decade to about 1730 was as described in the beginning of this chapter, the later style had the bodice shaped into the figure by a tighter-fitting lining. It was worn with all shapes of the hoops, the most popular being the pyramidal shape or fan hoop.

The separate bodice and skirt had three types of bodice: the casaquin, short basqued jacket bodice, close fitting to the waist, where it flared out over the petticoat in varying depths, with a square or round décolletage. It was fastened down the front to the waist, the laced fastenings concealed by a flap, it was not uncommon to see the jacket with a stomacher. The sleeves were the popular elbow length with plain or winged cuffs. The 'pet-en-l'air' was a jacket bodice loose fitting to thigh, or frequently to knee-length with a sack back. Robings were present and it was worn with a stomacher. The sleeves, like the casaquin style, were elbow length with plain or winged cuffs. Both styles of jacket bodice were worn with untrimmed petticoats over dome-shaped hoops, occasionally oblong hoops were used. The third type was the riding habit. This was made after the style of the male coat, side pleated vents with buttons, a back vent; like the man's coat it was without a collar. After 1730 there appeared a modification not worn by men and that was the joining of the front skirts to the body, giving a greater flare needed for the fuller petticoat. The sleeves were close-fitting and long to the wrist with closed cuffs. A waistcoat was worn which followed the man's style, this was darted at the sides to fit the smaller figure, or often this was a false garment being only front panels sewn to the coat lining. Similar to the men's style both the coat and the waistcoat had button fastening in the male fashion. The petticoat long and full often with inverted flounces.

Colours Fashionable colours for this period for gowns and petticoats were, blue, cherry, cinnamon, green, pink, purple, red, rose, scarlet and yellow.

Outdoor wear Fashionable as outdoor garments were the mantles and cloaks. The mantle, tent-like in shape to accommodate the hooped dresses, was long to the ground, and fitted with a hood and a large turned-down collar. The fastening was down the front with buttons from neck to hem. It was sleeveless with two large placket slits one on either side. The cloak was in varying lengths but usually about thigh length and worn generally without a hood.

Large Mob-cap c 1780

Dress accessories The term *handkerchief* was given at this period to ladies' neckwear. Although the pocket-handkerchief was also in common usage. The neckwear handkerchief was usually a large square of material, gauze, muslin, linen, lawn or silk, folded diagonally and placed round the neck, the long ends being secured in the front with ribbon ties. The handkerchiefs were often edged with lace matching the ruffles, if worn. They were often coloured in stripes, of a plain colour or with coloured spots. Black was used only for mourning.

The *modesty piece* was a strip of lace attached to the top border of the corset in the front and placed across the lower piece of the décolletage, it was not continued round the sides.

The *tucker* was a frilled edging for the low décolletage robe bodice carried up round the edges.

The *Steinkirk* was a male fashion taken up by the ladies with the riding habit and for informal wear. It consisted of a wide scarf of lawn or silk wrapped round the neck, the ends being twisted in the front, then pinned to the left side of the bodice. It came in various colours, reds, greens even gold.

Ribbon neck bands fitted closely round the neck high under the chin, hanging from the neck down over the bosom, usually of ruched ribbon.

Small mob-cap with lappets c 1785

Popular with the fashionable dresses was the ribbon girdle secured in the front with a knot or a jewelled buckle.

Aprons were considered as an elegant and decorative part of women's costume and for the more wealthy and fashionable were worn without bibs, for ordinary wear bibs were worn, used as a protective garment by the working women. As a fashion accessory they were either long or short, tied round the waist with running strings, threaded through the top hem. The long apron covered the front of the petticoat to the hem; often of a fine transparent material like muslin decorated with a floral or spotted design. The short apron was usually wider, about knee length, often of coloured silks, brocade or satin. Colours ranged from blue, black, green, pink, red, white or yellow.

Straw bergère hat c 1750

Large laced and feathered hat worn over large wig 1775

Pockets of this period were pear-shaped bags, made in pairs joined by tapes and worn under the dress being tied round the waist. They were reached through the placket slits on the side of the petticoat or skirt.

Headwear The high fontange white cap with its built-up laced pleats on the commode wire frame went out of fashion in the first decade. The headwear then took on a lower, closer to the head silhouette.

The pinner, which took over from the fontange, was a circular flat linen cap edged with a single or double frill, hanging down the back were two streamers or lappets, which were often turned up and pinned to the crown of the cap. Sometimes the lappets were tied under the chin and called kissing strings.

The coif, or round-eared cap, was bonnet shaped and framed the face level with the ears. The front of the cap had a single or double frill, the back being pulled in by a draw-string, this unfrilled back exposed the hair.

The mob cap was popular throughout the century, the puffed-out crown piece stood high towards the back of the head, a deep border framed the face with short lappets hanging down on either side. These were left hanging down or pinned under the chin completely framing the face and tied in this manner were called bridles. The borders were edged with lace.

Hats and hoods Day caps, which were the pinners, and mob-caps could on occasions be worn out of doors without any additional covering; usually, however, they were worn under hats or hoods. The hoods which were popular throughout the century could be separate or attached to a cloak. They were usually large and loose and made from a soft material. There were long hoods which had long streamers down either side which were crossed under the chin passed round the neck and secured behind, or just tied under the chin. The pug hood, also known as the short hood, was without the streamers and tied under the chin only, with coloured ribbons which matched the lining. The caped hood was made to be pleated round the neck and flared out to a flat shoulder collar, sometimes double.

The capuchin was a hood with a deep cape attached.

Hats from silk or straw were worn throughout the century often with low crowns and narrow brims trimmed with

Male fashions of the 1740s with the calf length coats and long waistcoats

ribbon or with low crowns and wide floppy brims. The Bergère hat, a large flat straw hat, was worn as fashion dictated throughout the century. It was secured to the head by ribbon ties which passed from the crown then over or under the brim then secured under the chin or behind the hair at the back.

For horse-riding, the three-cornered hat, similar to the men's style was worn, as also was the jockey hat.

The tall crowned hat with the wide flat brim was worn early in the century then became unfashionable and was worn only in the country.

Plain hairstyle with ringlets c 1729

Hairstyles Women's hairstyles at the beginning of the century were varied: the high tower hairstyle with its frizzed, built-up curls went out of fashion by the first decade. The simple hairstyle, worn by the ordinary working women, was adopted by the wealthy fashionable ladies and worn by them until about mid-century. It was a simple style with curls framing the face with the rest of the hair fashioned into a knot on the crown of the head.

The *Dutch coiffure* and the *tête de mouton* were both styles of simple coiffure with the front hair waved back with real or false clusters of ringlet curls at the back.

The German hairstyle, the Hanover cut, was similar to the earlier tower style and was a built-up hair on to pads structure, decorated with gauze and ribbon, and powdered with pomatum and powder. Although this had a certain popularity in Europe it did not become fashionable in England.

Wigs were not at this period fashionable and were worn only for riding, court or other special occasions.

Shoes remained pointed with the heels varying in height from 2 to 3 in. (5 to 8 cm). The high instep was covered by a square cut or scalloped tongue, fastened with buckles or latchets. Shoes were usually made from leather or brocade, the 'pattens' had wooden soles. After the 1730s the shoes became short-toed and had thinner heels often much lower than previously. Clogs when worn by the fashionable were worn as overshoes often being made in the same materials as the shoes they were covering. For inclement weather pattens were worn, these had wooden soles raised up on iron supports. The pattens were more used by country people.

Accessories Costume accessories are listed here although some may belong to the property department. *Stockings* which reached just above the knee, were knitted in various materials, from wool, yarn, cotton thread or silk. Garters were ribbon lengths tied just below the knee.

Elbow length *gloves* and mittens were very fashionable,

Front and back view of a coat with round cuffs and waist-coat c 1764

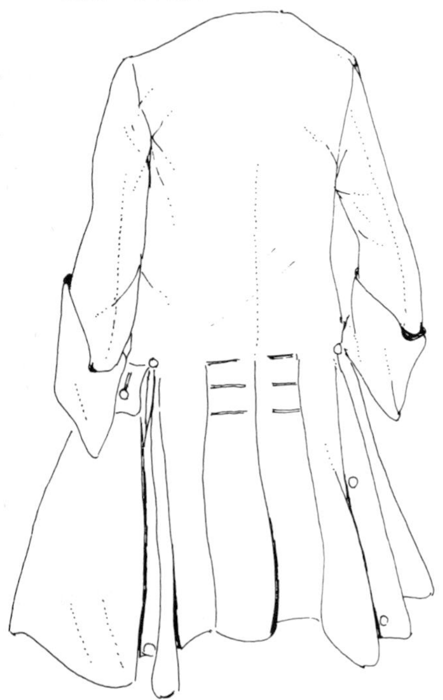

made in kid, cotton and silk. Small *muffs* were carried and were made in various materials such as fur, feathers and fabrics.

Fans of varying sizes and lace edged handkerchiefs were universally carried. Both *canes* and *umbrellas* were very popular and carried by the fashionable ladies. *Jewellery* was still extensively worn, but much of it was paste and false.

Artificial aids to fashion Cosmetics, such as rouge and white paint, were very much in vogue, and patches and powder still persisted. The use of plumpers remained in popularity as did the use of perfume and creams. Eyebrows were plucked often being supplemented by mouseskin.

Men's clothes The essential feature of men's dress consisting of coat, waistcoat and breeches, remained constant at the beginning of the eighteenth century and remained so for the following two generations or so.

Changing fads of fashion varied only in details of cut, the basic design remained. The expression of undress, formal or full dress merely meant the type of materials used. For undress or everyday wear materials like duffle, camlet, cloth, damask, cut velvet or satin were used. For formal full dress and court attire, gold and silver materials, brocades, heavily embroidered cloth and flowered velvets were more often used.

The coat The close-fitting coat for both dress and undress was shaped to the waist and continued down to a full-flared skirt which reached to just below the knees, although the length followed the taste of fashion at the time. The flared skirt of the coat had three vents from hip to hem, one either side with the side seams and the other in the centre of the back. The side vents, to produce the flare, were pleated with four pleats, then covered with decorative buttons. A greater flare effect was achieved by lining the pleats with a stiffening such as buckram, the back vent remained plain.

The neckline was usually without a collar and cut low in the front, after the second decade a small narrow upright band was occasionally worn. The coat fastened in a straight line down the front with a slight overlap of the skirts when it was fastened at the waist. The fastening was secured by means of buttons, usually dome shaped and covered in the same material as the coat. Metal buttons were also very popular. The early double-breasted coats were mainly worn by the military, but were also worn by the less fashionable middle and working classes.

The previous fashion of low placed pockets gave way in 1720 to a higher positioned pocket at just below waist level, and fitted with flaps, sometimes vertical but more often than not horizontal. The flaps had scalloped borders.

The loose-fitting sleeve after the first decade became closer-fitting and ended just above wrist level, allowing the full shirt sleeve to be revealed, the shirt sleeve had a closed band at the wrist and could be worn with or without a ruffle. The coat cuff itself varied in size and in style, those which were open behind were known as open sleeves. The closed cuffs or round cuffs were the most popular, both types were usually decorated with buttons and loops.

The *waistcoat* or vest, was cut on similar lines to the coat, close-fitting to the waist and flared skirts, the vents were unpleated. The skirt was cut some 3 to 4 in. (8 to 10 cm) shorter than the coat. The side vents were cut to form an acute angle at the hem, the back vent was slit to the shoulder then laced to fit the wearer. The back of the waistcoat was usually made in a cheaper material (as it was not seen) than the foreparts or fronts. The neckline was without a collar, and fastened from neck to hem line with slightly smaller buttons than the coat. Buttons were sometimes covered by a fly flap, although this seemed to be mainly a French fashionable method.

Collarless long coat and waistcoat with buttons from neck to hem c 1739

The waistcoat pockets followed the style of the coat but were smaller. The sleeves, when present, were close-fitting to the arm and were without cuffs, worn usually with a back slit at the wrist with a button fastening. When worn as a lounge jacket indoors, the waistcoat was made with both back and foreparts of the same material. Double-breasted waistcoats were worn usually being fastened at the waist only allowing the top to be turned over to form lapels.

Breeches The style of breeches remained unchanged throughout the eighteenth century and were universally worn by all classes. They were cut with a very wide angle at the fork, the back being very full and gathered into a waistband, then allowed to hang round the hips. The legs narrowed towards the knee and finished just below the

Waistcoat of 1745-50

knee in a kneeband.

The knees were covered by stockings which were pulled over the breeches, the more fashionable began to wear the kneeband fastened just below the knee and over the stocking, both were in usage until the middle of the century. The waistband was wider in the front than the back and was fastened by three cloth covered buttons. At the back of the breeches was a slit opening with eyelet holes on either side for laces which closed the waistband to suit the waist of the wearer. Later in the period a strap with a buckle adjustment was in use. The waistband in this period was the only means of supporting the breeches.

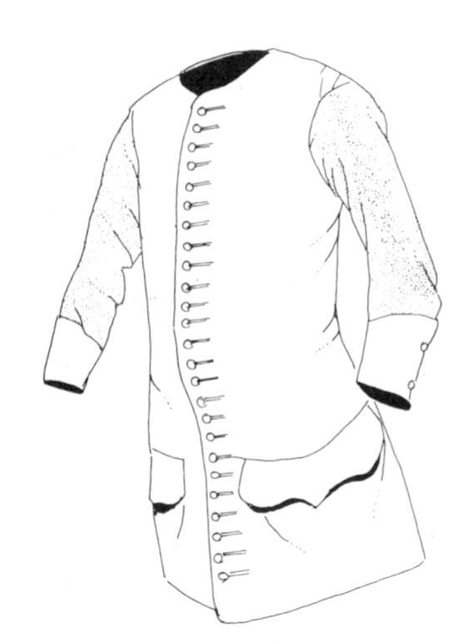

Waistcoat with plain sleeves 1720

British soldier of the Guards in a three-cornered hat and a British Grenadier officer in mitre hat 1745-1751

Group of American colonists during the Indian Wars of 1754

Frock In this period the working-class men wore a garment known as a 'frac' or 'frock' for the protection of their clothes. This loose-fitting garment was a buttoned down the front type of coat with a flat turned-down collar; made usually in coarse twill, sacking and ticking. This was taken up by the gentlemen of fashion and made from a woollen material, because of its comfort and freedom of movement it became the ordinary wear for gentlemen. By the end of the century

Man with headcloth c 1750

it was called the 'frock coat'. The sleeves ended near the wrist in a round closed cuff which was usually very deep and wide, also worn was the short slit type sleeve.

Leisure wear for gentlemen of this period was the night-gown, a long loose fitting garment with a wrap-over front tied round the waist with a sash. The sleeves were long and loose-fitting. Other variations of mens negligee were the closer-fitting morning gown and the loose house coat which ended just below the knees called a 'banyan'. All three were made in brocades, damask, silk or satin.

Outdoor wear Cloaks at this time were still commonly worn although by the mid-century the cloak ceased to be fashionable. It was a full loose garment, the gathered neck piece was hidden under the flat turned-down collar which was secured under the chin by a clasp fastening. It was long to the knees and had a slit vent at the back for horse-riding. Other variations of the cloak had double cape collars and had front fastening with buttons.

Coming into fashionable wear for outdoor garments was the 'surtout' or great coat. The design followed the dress coat but naturally was much larger and looser. The skirt was flared although with less pleats at the side vents, which was often absent with only a narrow slit to accommodate a sword on the left side. It had a double cape collar, the upper collar being smaller could be turned up and buttoned down the front, occasionally a small standing collar was substituted in place of the upper small collar. The great coat was buttoned from neck to hem but more often was fastened only up to the waist. It had a back vent as this coat was worn for horse-riding.

Neckwear The earlier falling collar had now been replaced by the neckcloth which basically was a strip of material about 1 ft wide and 3 ft long (30 cm x 90 cm), this was placed round the neck and knotted in front. The variations were in the manner of tying it, each had its own special name. The cravat was a strip of linen, lawn or muslin worn round the neck and loosely tied under the chin. A Steinkirk was a lace cravat very loosely tied in front, with the ends passed through a buttonhole or pinned on one side of the coat. It was named after the Battle of Steenkerque, where French officers were caught unawares and had to go into battle without being able to adjust their cravats properly;

this was a popular fashion both in France and England regardless of the fact that it was an English defeat. It was little worn after mid-century. The stock was a piece of linen pleated into a high neckband with a stiffener. It was secured by a buckle at the back. The military usually wore a black stock but this was often copied by the young dandies and bucks of the day. The solitaire was a black broad ribbon tied to the running strings of a bag-wig, the ends being arranged in various ways. The ordinary workman usually wore a pleated handkerchief knotted in front.

Large full bottom wig c 1709

Wigs Universally the wig supplanted natural hair, this remarkable feature was worn by all fashionable gentility. The natural hair was cut very short or even shaven very close. The earliest and most elaborate of the period was the full-bottom wig, worn in various forms until the 1730s then, due to its inconvenience and costly maintenance, it went out of fashion and was then worn only by professional men and at court. At first it was made into three divisions of massed curls, two in front (one either side) and one hanging down the back. The wig then rose into two horns, sometimes in exaggerated forms, one either side of a centre parting. After the second decade the wig was shortened and the curls were tied back forming the tye wig worn for undress and by graduate students.

The military fashion of enclosing the back hair into a bag of gummed black taffeta with a bow, became a popular civilian fashion called the bag-wig. The campaign wig, often called a travelling wig as it was usually worn by soldiers or when riding on horseback, had a centre parting with bushy hair and curls on either side these locks were turned up and tied into a knot.

The bob wig worn by all classes was worn as an undress wig and varied as a long bob which covered the neck, or as a short bob which exposed the neck. The scratch wig and the cut wig were both of minimum size and used for business and sports.

The Ramillies wig was worn mainly by the military personnel, but sometimes by the beaux wishing to affect a military air.

Full bottom wig c 1700

The pigtail was almost as popular as the military bag-wig due to its convenience of not having the larger wig flapping over the face and neck. Wigs with this sort of 'queue' as it was referred to, introduced the toupee, or hair over the

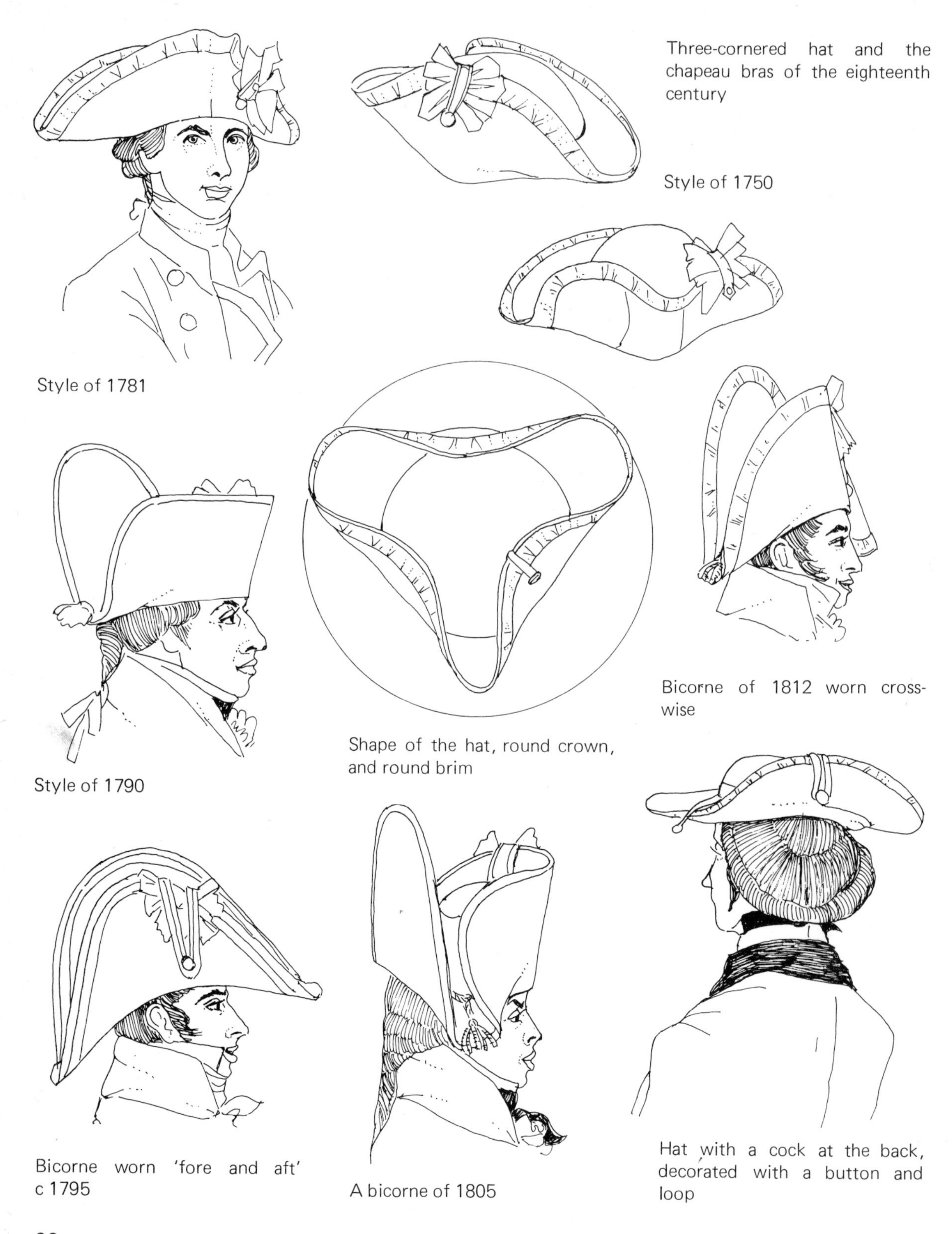
Three-cornered hat and the chapeau bras of the eighteenth century
Style of 1750
Style of 1781
Bicorne of 1812 worn crosswise
Style of 1790
Shape of the hat, round crown, and round brim
Bicorne worn 'fore and aft' c 1795
A bicorne of 1805
Hat with a cock at the back, decorated with a button and loop

Early bag-wig type c 1751

forehead, which was often natural, this was brushed back to form a roll over each temple. The join of the natural hair intermingling with the wig was plastered with pomatum and then disguised with a liberal use of powder which was then applied all over. The extraordinary vogue in fashion of covering the hair with white powder seems to have continued almost the greater part of the eighteenth century. The natural hair was, for economy sake, dressed in various ways to represent wigs; being also heavily powdered. Workmen often wore their own hair long if they did not wear a wig.

Wigs were not always made of human hair, as this was expensive. Horse hair, goats' hair, mohair, and foxes' tails were often substituted. Copper and iron wire was also used.

Headwear Because of the widespread and universal use of wigs, headwear played a very insignificant part in fashionable modes. Hats were no longer worn indoors and were more often than not carried under the arm.

The three-cornered hat was the most popular. The crown was deep, flat or rounded, with wide brims which were cocked, that is, turned up on three sides, standing away from the crown, worn with a point in the front. The brim was usually edged with a braid or open lace work; for dress wear a button and loop decorated the left cock.

Military hats were worn with a high turned-up brim with deep laced edgings and a black cockade. The civilian hat of this type was the 'Kevenhuller' style. Fashionable, when worn, were a variety of styles and names, such as Dettingen a military style, the Monmouth cock, already unfashionable at this period, had only the back cocked, then the small cocked, large cock, laced hat, open cock! Many were laced and feathered.

The exception to the three-cornered hat was that worn by clergymen and workers who wore the 'round' hat with the uncocked brim. The brim was either rigid, as worn by the professional men, or slouched for the working man. Hats continued to be made from beaver or, for the not so wealthy classes, coney and rabbit, felt and straw. The latter for the round hat in the countryside.

Footwear The square blocked-toe shoes with the high square heels remained in fashion; the shoe uppers covered the foot and ended in square tongues which rose high in front of the ankle. The sides were closed and the shoes, which fastened by straps from the heel leathers, were usually buckled over the tongues. This high-tongue shoe style was affected by the military, from which this fashion came, the dandies and fops of the period exaggerated them and wore them very high.

Heavy jackboots, light jackboots, half jackboots and jockey boots were mainly worn by the army or for travelling, riding and hunting.

Stockings were mostly knitted either by hand or machine and came in various colours and materials.

Accessories Again, although the costume accessories are listed, some may belong to the property department rather than to the wardrobe.

Gloves and mittens were either carried or worn, high gauntlet type gloves which came above the wrist had a slit behind which was usually trimmed with a fringe, these were very fashionable at the time. *Muffs* still retained their popularity but were now either medium or small in size. Swords were still carried by 'gentlemen', and hung from a frog hooked to a sword belt from under the vest. The hilt of the sword protruded from the left side vent of the coat. From the hilt of the sword was often a sword knot which was a bunch of highly coloured decorative ribbons. Pistols had taken over as a weapon of defence and therefore the sword remained purely as a decorative accessory.

From the beginning of the century *canes* of all sizes were carried; the knobs or heads of the canes were usually very elaborate, made of precious metal such as gold and silver and semi-precious stones including agate and amber. The knobs could be unscrewed and the cavity contained many novel ideas, from scent to mirrors. Carved heads and figures came into vogue with the heavy oak sticks. Heavy *cudgels* were also carried by the workers and the unfashionable. The canes were carried in the hand, tied to the third button of the coat or attached by a loop to the wrist or finger.

Artificial aids to fashion The dandies and the beaux of this period were as interested in artificial aids to beauty as the ladies. The use of rouge for the face and lips, patches, padding for padded calves, perfume and powder was in common usage. They carried ornate watches and snuff-boxes.

Late Georgian

This so called Gallant Epoch had one great characteristic, its exaggeration in all things. The superficial mask of the Rococo period included both architecture and fashionable costume which concerns the stage designer most.

This lack of moderation showed up sharply in the over lavish decoration and irregularity of form which was reflected in this violent and contrasting period of history. Historically it was an age of revolution intermingled with a false air of 'an age of elegance'. The two lived together

Woman in closed robe and shawl-cloak, buffon. The man on the left is in a plain frock coat with turned down collar and short waistcoat. The man on the right is in a collarless coat with cuffs à la marinière c 1775

Man in long frock coat, buckled breeches and slippers. Short waistcoat, three-cornered hat, walking cane, medium muff c 1780
Lady in short polonaise, large lace hat with banging chignon. The skirt was flounced around the hem c 1780

in a period of uneasy alliance with an increasing extravagance of styles from the French court which influenced European fashion. The zenith of these fashions was reached when the high coiffures became even higher, the width of the hoop made walking a most difficult, unnatural function, and when ornamentation became more artificial and fantastic.

With new inventions many more types of textiles were brought into common usage: Hargreaves' Spinning Jenny, Arkwright's cotton-spinning loom, Cartwright's weaving loom and Watt's steam engine in the cotton factories, caused a growth in the weaving centres. The Industrial Revolution began to gain for England the world markets, and the cotton materials brought about a great change in European clothing. With these changes in industry other countries were affected in greater or lesser degrees, especially in this period.

After the independence of America, and the opening of free trading of American ports, Spain increased her trade and in consequence Spanish costume reached southern Latin America.

War brought about a lessening of Holland's industries which halted the extension of its fashion. Belgium, Rhine-

Man in frock coat with the military style turned back lapels. French top boots, short waist-coat c 1775
Young lady in a jacket, 'pet en l'air' style, turned up winged cuffs, half sleeves, petticoat and stomacher. Mob-cap c 1775

Young girl's hairstyle of 1789

Natural hair with curls c 1790

land and Saxony expanded their outputs of linen, cotton, silks and velvets. Switzerland too increased the production of cotton, silks and ribbons. Italy took no great part in this revival of industry, after becoming part of the possessions of the Hapsburgs. Bavaria and Austria remained predominately active in agriculture.

It is important for the historical stage costume designer to note how this unequal sharing of industrial prosperity had an effect on the influence of fashion. A great wave of Anglomania swept France and other European countries, its influence initially could be seen in the men's costume which followed the pastoral fashion, the typical English innovation and vogue for informal country garments. English women's clothing also profited from the progress and ideas and economical development of the industrial conditions. The introduction of the gown à l'anglaise, superseded the *robe à la française* for everyday wear, leaving the French gown for ceremonial purposes only.

Extreme exaggerated styles as in all periods, showed themselves first in the guise of the Macaronis, a fashionable group of Englishmen. The main characteristic of this set were their large egg-shaped wigs and the ridiculous small three-cornered hat perched on top of the wig. This was followed post Revolution, by an essentially French style exaggeration of the Incroyables (as the name suggests) and the female counterpart, the Merveilleuses. Both costumes caricatured the prevailing modern innovations of the English countryman's clothes and the classic transparent models of antiquity.

The whole century was consumed with war and talk of war, therefore uniforms were very much a part of everyday life. These I have placed into their respective periods in illustration rather than in the text, as they would need volumes of their own to describe them.

The French Revolution came terrifyingly and violently, sweeping aside like a large gigantic tidal wave all the past traditions and social disparities. The political and economical scene changed, and as in all crises, the modes of fashion followed the ever-changing pattern of fortune.

With the ending of the French Court's social life, the distinction of social standing in France by costume was abolished by the National Assembly in May 1789. This, as in other events throughout history, was a further turning-point in the ever-changing face of fashion and costume.

Man in coat and waistcoat of embroidered material. Typical small round cuffs c 1770
The women in open robes and large hats. Front lady is wearing an écharpe cloak (a broad long scarf) c 1780

Women's fashion From the middle of the eighteenth century, the robes of the fashionable ladies remained somewhat similar to the previous half without its ponderous affiliation to the early Rococo style. Modification and exaggerated variation took over the female fashion costume.

The gown The sack dress which had started the eighteenth century was now known as the *robe à la français* and was worn for dress and undress but was essentially an open robe. Until the 1760s the open bodice type had a wide spread décolletage with a buttoned false front stomacher, the robings being carried down to the hem, this was usually worn as undress. From the 1770s waistcoats were sometimes worn.

The closed bodice sack dress was worn without robings with an edge to edge concealed closure, this type often being referred to as full dress. Variations to the sack-back consisted of allowing the pleats to hang from the shoulders to the hips without being attached to the bodice, the pleats then merged with the overskirt, or the pleats were joined to the bodice at the waist, then again merging with the overskirt.

The *robe à l'anglaise* with the characteristic feature of the *corsage en fourreau* remained in fashion until well into the 1780s. Variations in the open bodice which was without robings was worn with false waistcoat or zone sewn on to the

Close hairstyle intermingled with flowers c 1807

Ladies in the French court dress. They were high waisted in the open robe style. Lady on the left has an extremely long and narrow train. The lady on the right has a smaller trained overskirt. Both dresses had low décolletages surrounded by a lace edging. They wore close-fitting bonnets with feather decorations c 1803

Lace headwear and shoulder shawl c 1795

inner lining of the bodice. Sleeve variation followed from the elbow length with round cuffs or flounces to the long three-quarter length with a small ruffle. The principal styles of women's costume were now introduced first with the polonaise which remained in fashion in one form or the other for some fifteen years. Its characteristic feature being the three panniers, one at the back and one either side, which were rounded at the front, the short version with these bunched up draperies exposed the petticoat all round, this was more popular than the long version which came into fashion a little later. The arrangement of the overskirt to produce these drapes of puffed contours, was by running cords which were anchored at the hem, then threaded through rings up each seam to the waist. The cords had tassel ends. Later the puffs were sewn into position with a bow of ribbon between the puffs. The petticoat, which exposed the ankles, was usually decorated with a wide flounce round the hem, but a quilted petticoat was also worn sometimes.

The *bodice* without robings was worn either with a low square or round neckline with a breast knot fastening or secured with an edge to edge front fastening. At the back the bodice fitted the figure closely and continued into the overskirt without a seam. The front gap was filled with either a waistcoat or a zone. Sleeves varied from the elbow length with round cuffs or frills, three-quarter length with a frill or long to the wrist and fastened with buttons. The long 'polonaise' although basically the same in every way with the exception that it had a long trained overskirt. A variation of the polonaise was the 'circassian' which had three panniers of equal length and an edge to edge closure on the bodice. The sleeves were short over the long close-fitting sleeves of the undergarment.

In the 1780s the *bustle look* returned with the use of artificial padding, this false rump was often a padded cork contraption that fitted at the back of the waist. This was used with the open robe style of dress, the most popular being the 'Levite' although following the style of the polonaise, it was not drawn up, the effect was achieved by the cork bustle.

The closed robe became very popular again in the 1780s the chemise variation was made from a very light material with a close-fitting bodice with a low round neckline edged with a vandyked falling collar. The dress was closed from bosom to hem by a series of buttons or coloured bows.

Country working girl of the period. Soldier in frock coat with turned back lapel. Short gaiters. Epaulette on left shoulder. Three-cornered hat c 1781

Simple classical hairstyle c 1800

The sleeves were long and close fitting to the arm and buttoned at the wrist. The skirt, long to the ground, was gathered to the waist of the bodice, often flounced at the hem. A broad sash was placed round the waist and tied at the back the ends dangling down the back.

At the same time there was an interesting development with the *women's riding and travelling costume*, it was also popular as a morning walking dress. It was based on the men's fashion of the day. The bodice fitted close to the body, the neck finishing with a double or treble deep collar with broad lapels. Although open at the neck it could be buttoned up or filled in with a muslin 'buffon'.

For riding, only the women's costume consisted of a hip-length jacket and a short waistcoat, both with wide turned-back collars. The open-breasted front was covered with a cravat secured at the throat with a masculine bow. This was worn with a multi-petticoated, bell-shaped skirt which fell

5

Large loose turban style hat over large hairstyle c 1785

A French Incroyable with enormous neckcloth, short double breasted jacket with bulky pleats at the back and lapels. Breeches with mid calf boots of soft leather c 1794

to the ground. The separate bodice and skirt type was always worn as undress. The bodice was now always worn as a jacket which had a close-fitting bodice with a low cut neck and a deep skirt either hip or thigh length, other variations were worn with the sack or fourreau backs. It was closed down the front in various ways, lacing, hooks and eyes or even a false front, waistcoats were not uncommon. Sleeves were either the elbow length or long to the wrist. They had such names as 'French jacket' or the 'pet-en-l'air' or 'Caraco'. The latter was always in reference to a thigh-length close-fitting jacket with flare skirts, and worn with a petticoat over dome or oblong hoops, a girdle was worn either over or under the jacket.

The *négligée* was always worn as undress and although sometimes referred to as a 'nightgown' it was worn at public places and at home, weddings and funerals. It was made of a fine material in the open robe with stomacher style. At home it was worn without the hoop. The Italian style robe was a much more fashionable négligée, with low décolletage bodice without robings fastened down the front with edge to edge closure finishing in a deep point, the back was close-fitting with a whalebone stiffener in each of the four seams, the sleeves were elbow length with round cuffs. The overskirt was pleated to the bodice waist with the opening in the front. The petticoat was usually of a different colour.

The French revolution period

The *French Revolution* of 1789 was a turning point in the historical costume history. As Paris was the arbiter of the fashionable Western world the effect was reflected everywhere. Perhaps more so in women's costume and the movement towards a greater simplicity was shown by the complete abandonment of hoops, petticoats, corsets, and a closer link with the freedom of ancient Greece.

The general silhouette now became elongated with the banishing of the bustles and protrusions. White transparent high-waisted dresses of muslin were in fashion with and without underclothing. At this period of 1790s the dress moved towards a greater simplicity and freedom especially in France where this new found freedom was expressed by the new Parisian trend setters called the 'Merveilleuses', under the guidance of Mesdames Recamier and Tallien.

Figures of the French Revolution, a soldier of the period. Woman with the tricolour sash. The centre figure after Bouilly (an artist of that time) is the sans culotte baggy pantaloons, double breasted waistcoat, short jacket c 1789

The man on the left is wearing the casual dress of a hunting gentleman, his cocked hat askew in a rakish fashion, c 1760. The lady is in flimsy white muslin, in the highwaisted fashion of c 1805. To the right is a revolutionist in the dress of 1790, a short 'carmagnole' peasant jacket and red felt 'phrygian' cap ornamented with the tri-color cockade. He carries a long staffed pike

The man on the left is dressed in the style of the American colonists of 1774. The hat is uncocked. Woollen stockings were often worn. The lady is wearing a version of the 'short polonaise', and a powdered wig with a large gauze cap on top, 1778. To the right is a fashionable dandy of the day in striped coat and stockings with a high cocked hat, 1788

Group of Merveilleuse and Incroyables. Raggedly cut hair hanging over ears. Faces masked with oversized neckcloths. Exaggerated lapels, three-quarter length frock coats. The central figure is wearing breeches with long body and short fall. The Merveilleuse wears a long flimsy dress, the hem draped over the arm. Ribboned headdress and short cloak

Man in single breasted overcoat with 'M' shaped lapels over frock coat and double waistcoat fashion, high stock cravat. Breeches with deep cuffed top boots, beaver top hat c 1807

Centre woman wearing an outdoor dress with turned down collar fastened down the front, sleeves long and close fitting. She is wearing the capote style bonnet. Boas over the shoulders c 1807

Woman on the left wearing a pelisse long to the ground with broad turned down collar with tippet c 1803

A Merveilleuse in the robe en chemise with an outside neckcloth, full long skirt pulled up c 1794

The Merveilleuses To the stage costume historical designer this represents a complete break-away from all the previous fashions. This robe 'en chemise', as it was called, was more akin to the previous decades' underwear and similar to the dress of the ancient Egyptian ladies it was more a state of undress than dress.

It was from the earlier discovery of Pompeii and Herculaneum that inspired the French women to accept all things Classical, and the styles of the Ancient Greeks and Romans were copied with perhaps more superficial resemblance than reality. Nonetheless these styles were taken up and imitated throughout Europe.

The *basic dress* was a flimsy chemise of transparent muslin, the bodice was gathered at the neck and under the breasts and joined in one to the skirt, which gave an extremely short waist line. The décolletage varied considerably but at this early period of the sheer muslin gown the Merveilleuses wore it very low revealing more of the bosom than concealing. The waist was encircled by a slim ribbon girdle. The skirt was long to the ground fairly close-fitting, the excess material from the hem was draped up and carried over the arm, thus revealing a great deal of leg. The wearing of an underskirt or flesh coloured tights was at the discretion of the wearer, which in the case of the Merveilleuses whose intention appears to shock the conservative habits of the past, they went bare armed, bare backed, no tights and wore only flimsy laced Grecian sandals. The colour of the gown was mainly in white although light pastel shades were worn.

Large brimmed hat with low crown, ribbon decorated over laced cap c 1799

The Merveilleuses wore their *hair* long and in a neglected state with a ragged fringe over the forehead. The extraordinary *headwear* affected by these ladies among many was the poking-hat, it had an enormous brim, not unlike the English jockey hat, which extended brim stood high off the forehead.

The *Incroyables* were freakish untidy dandies of France in the last decade of the eighteenth century. They wore large outsize neckclothes which partially concealed and sometimes completely hid the lower part of the face. The stiff shirt collar was turned up inside the cravat the points being in view against the jaw line. The coats were knee length often of striped wool with extremely wide lapels with an equally wide brocade lining. The close fitting breeches were buttoned at the knee and ended with bows knotted and the ends allowed to dangle down over the stockings. The hair was straggly and unkempt crowned with a bicorne hat with the tricolour rosette as decoration, sometimes they wore the English type jockey boots. Usually they carried a short cudgel stick in preference to the more elegant cane.

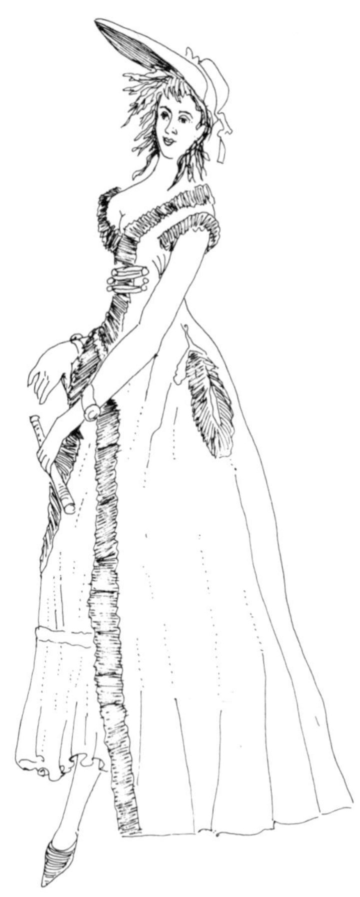
A Merveilleuse in the open robe style fur trimmed, and the poking bonnet with an enormous brim c 1794

Classical style gowns At this period all gowns were high waisted with longer skirts. Two styles emerged with the gown and petticoat type and the gown-over-gown style, both in the open robe vogue.

Gown and petticoat The bodice was short with a wrap-over front usually with a low décolletage with the roll 'Capuchin collar', the bodice being secured at the waist with ties or buttons which were concealed by a ribbon girdle. The back of the bodice was cut to allow for the deep inserting of the sleeve armholes giving it a very narrow appearance. The trained overskirt was open from the high wrap-over in an inverted V-shape opening which revealed the petticoat, ground length and untrained. The sleeves were either three-quarter length with a light half sleeve or long to the wrist.

Gown-over-gown The bodice of the overgown had a low décolletage tied or laced in front with the under gown revealed above it. The overskirt which was little more than a broad tail piece was trained, being a contrasting colour to the underskirt. The sleeves were either long to the wrist or half sleeves which revealed the long sleeves of the under-dress.

These dresses remained basically as described but as with all fashion many minor modifications took place.

Classical hairstyle c 1803

The round gown The chemise gown, as this style was also called, was a high waisted muslin cambric or calico garment which fell to the ground and was sometimes so transparent that it was necessary to wear tights underneath. The Merveilleuses who wore this type of dress would dampen the material so that it clung closer to the body to imitate the folds of the ancient Greek dresses seen on antique statues. Other variations were the dress in one which, in my opinion is an easier garment to make for stage purposes. This had a draw string at the neck, another below the bosom and they could be drawn in and draped at will. The modifications to this type of dress were that the neck became lower and the waist, as shown by the draw string, came closer up to the

High crowned poke bonnet secured with ribbons and a betsie collar c 1805

bosom. The sleeves were short, sometimes these were non-existent, and the train became longer. A separate bodice was reintroduced and was sewn on to the dress, it was as short as it was possible to be and very low in front. It was fastened either at the back or the front, the fastening being hidden under a piece of material.

Outdoor wear The cloak continued to be the main form for women's outdoor garments. The variations and names were allocated to widely different styles. The *long cloak* enveloped the whole body and was fitted with a cape-like hood which was ideal for winter. The *shawl* cloak was only deep to the waist crossed over in the front and tied behind, the ends were allowed to dangle down the back of the petticoat. The *écharpe-cloak* was somewhat like a modern stole, which went round the shoulders and the ends hung down from the shoulders on either side to hem length. The *pelisse* was a long to calf length hooded cloak with two

Man servant in the short frock, short straight across waistcoat and pantaloons. Lady of quality in muslin high waisted round gown with large muff, 'handkerchief'. Full dress bonnet c 1785

Man in the English type country clothes, bob-tail frock coat, short square waistcoat with lapels. Knee breeches and stockings. High beaver top hat. The young lady is wearing the high waisted dress of cambric c 1810

Long loose hanging hairstyle falling over the shoulders c 1791

Close hairstyle built over a pad c 1792

vertical slits for the arms. By the end of the century the pelisse had completely changed its silhouette, when it became a high waisted overcoat. The *cardinal* and the *polonese* were small hooded cloaks, as also was the *boisson*. The *handkerchiefs* were in fact small shoulder capes.

Coats These became fashionable in the late 1780s when the gowns began to discard the hoops. The *great coat* was three-quarter length and worn with a girdle, used mainly for riding and walking. The *spencer* was a short-waisted coat without skirts, it was close-fitting with a roll collar and sleeve long to the wrist, very popular with the muslin dresses during inclement weather. *Shawls* made their appearance in the 1780s, and made from cotton and silk were very fashionable.

Dress accessories *The neckerchief* continued to be worn as the most popular and fashionable neck covering until the end of the century, the term covered most of the varieties of neck coverings, of which there were many. In the

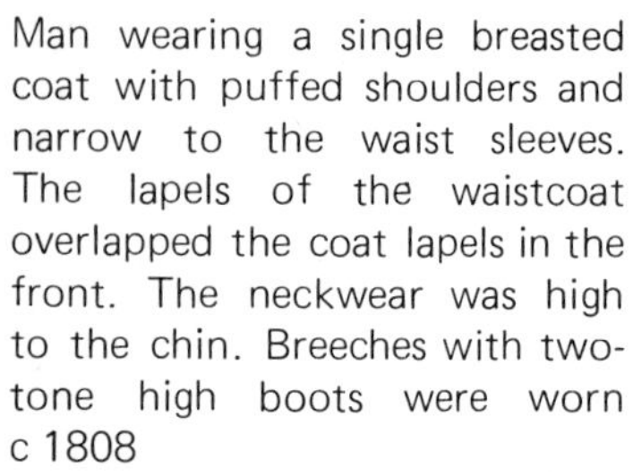

Man wearing a single breasted coat with puffed shoulders and narrow to the waist sleeves. The lapels of the waistcoat overlapped the coat lapels in the front. The neckwear was high to the chin. Breeches with two-tone high boots were worn c 1808

1750s it draped the décolletage, crossed over forming a V-shape in front, then tied behind. By the 1770s it was larger and covered the neck and shoulders and the 1780s saw it as a large 'buffon' which covered the neck and shoulders and puffed up over the décolletage.

The *muff* was worn throughout the second half of the century, often as a narrow frill round the neck leaving the

Lady in mob-cap with ribbon band, curled ringlets and hair hanging down the back. Round gown with flounced hem. Low décolletage, wide ribbon waist-band tied at the back with dangling ends. Sailor in short jacket, waistcoat, baggy pantaloons, low crowned wide brimmed hat

Large brimmed hat with enormous ribbon hatband c 1789

Large picture Gainsborough hat decorated with feathers c 1775

low décolletage uncovered. The larger ruff was a deep three tier cape falling over the shoulders from a close-fitting neckband, and was popular in the 1780s. It had an edge to edge join at the front. The *tippet*, rather like a fichu in shape, covering the shoulders secured in front and the ends allowed to hang in front. The *tucker* continued to be worn throughout the century, but the *modesty piece* went out of fashionable wear in the 1760s. The ribbon neck-band was popular, continuing well into the next century. *Aprons* of muslin, gauze, silk and lawn were worn until the early 1790s when they became unfashionable and were then worn only for domestic purposes.

Hoops The use of the hoop lasted until about 1785 then became discarded although they continued to be worn at court until the second decade of the nineteenth century.

Headwear Head covering was common throughout the century for indoors although with fashion there were exceptions. The small round caps and the round-eared cap gradually went out of fashion in the 1760s. The popular headwear during the last half of the century was the Dormeuse which lasted until the 1790s. This large crowned caul type cap fitting loosely over the head had side flaps of lace turned back from the temples exposing the front hair and forehead, trimmed with ribbon bows. The general cap shape between the 70s and 80s consisted of a large puffed up crown with a frill or narrow lappets, a trailing streamer down the back from the cap was very common and fashionable. From the early 1790s the wearing of day caps became unfashionable except for the elderly. Outdoor headwear during this period was very varied. The *calash*, was a large folding hood with a short cape attached; it was built on an arched-shape cane structure covered over with silk. The advantage of this hood was that it was able to protect and cover the very changeable massive fashionable coiffures. The most popular hat of the period was the milkmaid or Bergère hat, this lasted in various guises, large and small throughout. It followed the vagaries of the fashionable hairstyles. During this period women adopted a wide range of headwear from small to large, too numerous to mention, these were followed by the bonnet fashion, predominantly straw they were in the main of reasonable proportions and fastened under the chin with ribbon.

Large hat with ribbon decoration c 1796

Wig and hairstyle decorated with ribbon and feathers c 1782

Lunardi type hat c 1789

Hairstyles Women's hairstyles in the 1750s were low and neat, by the 60s they began to rise up in height and in the 70s reaching enormous heights, becoming wider in the 80s and, by the 1790s, they became again more natural to suit the changing fashions of a changing world. In the late 1760s came exaggerated arrangements of towering hairstyles in excess of 3 feet (1 metre). These were achieved by building over pads of horse-hair. The basic style was a mass of stiff hair-rolls rising to a peak; it was then plastered with pomatum and powered white. By the 1780s it was less high but became wider, this fashion, however, was short-lived and there was a rapid return to more natural styles. As this is such a vast subject I would again suggest that the costume designer should research this aspect thoroughly. A good 'make-up' person in the team is most essential.

Shoes Women's shoes remained very much the same over the whole period, they continued to be made in leather, brocade or satin, with ornamental buckles. Overshoes were the high pattens, with clogs for the poorer people.

Accessories *Gloves* usually of elbow length were worn, made from muslin, kid and cotton. *Muffs* of moderate size were always fashionable, becoming larger in the 1780s until the end of the century, made from various materials, furs, and fabrics decorated with ribbons. By the end of 1790 the *handbag* replaced the pocket, these were called ridicules or indispensibles. *Masks* became unfashionable and were discarded in the late 1760s. *Nosegays* in bosom bottles were very fashionable. *Jewellery* remained very much as previously stated in the first half of the century.

Artificial aids to fashion The use of rouge still persisted, although white paint was now discarded. Face patches were worn until the 1790s. Eyebrows were plucked and false bosoms were worn.

Men's coats The coat remained close fitting unwaisted with no flaring skirt after the 1760s. The collar made its appearance in the late 1760s increasing in height over the years. The curving away from the waistline was very prominent by the 1770s. After 1760 the fastening or button and button hole arrangements were from neck to waist, the military coat with the narrow lapels from neck to waist and turned back were adapted to civilian wear. Sleeves were long to the wrist fairly close fitting with the shirt ruff emerging. Cuffs were present in various forms, round, open and *à la marinière*, a sham cuff was worn in the 1790s.

Waistcoat The *waistcoat* consisted of a pair of foreparts and a back lining. Sleeves were now discarded. The two styles persisted throughout the period. The single breasted remained throughout, but the double breasted was unusual in the 1750s, 60s and 70s, very popular in the 80s, and most fashionable in the 90s. Under waistcoats also came into fashion in the 1790s and appeared above the turned back lapel of the overwaistcoat.

High wig coiffure with silk mobcap c 1776

High wig decorated with ribbon and feathers c 1776

Sailor and young working girls. Sailor wearing blue short jacket, white wide pantaloons, three-cornered hat and enormous pigtail c 1780

Double breasted waistcoat c 1780

Lady in male style riding habit of high waisted short tailed frock coat with flat turned down collar. Single breasted waistcoat, plain petticoat, high crowned narrow brimmed hat c 1790

Man in frock coat with lapels, double breasted waistcoat, cravat, natural hair and high crowned hat. English jockey top boots of soft leather c 1795

British grenadier in sloping away coat and turned back lapels. Short gaiters and ticking stockings

Indian brave in background. Man (right) in buckskin 'wamus' with self fringing. Leather skins, black felt hat c 1775

A French dragoon in the uniform of the period. Frock coat with buttoned back lapels narrow sleeves, high standing collar, straight across short waistcoat. Breeches and high reinforced topped boots. Brass helmet in the neo-classical style. Small tuft (aigrette) at the front, falling 'mane' of black horsehair, feathered plume c 1806

Lady in a close fitting separate bodice jacket with a short basque at the back. Frilled tippet gives the pouter-pigeon look. High close fitting ribbon hat c 1796

Child in a long high waisted muslin dress c 1804

Man on left in long frock coat with stand-fall collar, single breasted waistcoat striped stockings and chapeau bras c 1790
Man in a long redingote buttoned to the waist. Soft high leather boots. High crown and wide brimmed hat and a long muff c 1789

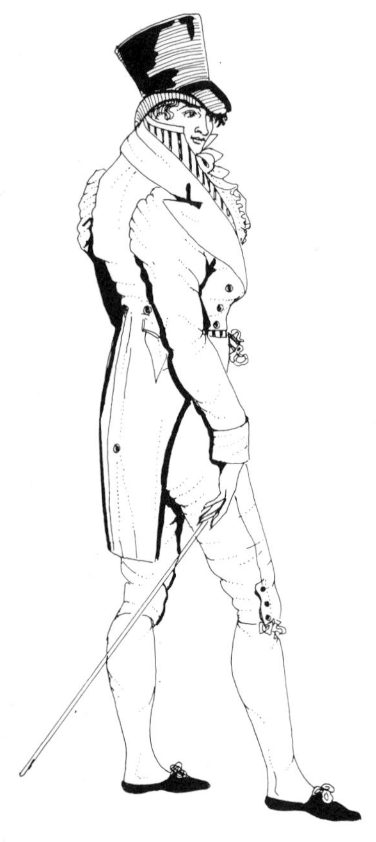

Man above in a double breasted coat cut back to form a tail-coat, the back was divided into two tails, the deep lapel had an 'M' cut. The sleeves had puffed shoulders. The waistcoat had a high stiff collar. He wore breeches, stockings and slipper shoes. High beaver top-hat c 1807

Breeches continued to be made as in the previous half of the century, with the notable exception that they were now becoming a closer fit. The knee band was now worn fastened just below the knee and over the stocking for all fashionable wear. The Macaronis, the dandies of the 1770s, usually wore ribbons instead of the breeches' buckles. *Pantaloons* were worn from early 1790 onwards, they were close fitting tights following the contours of the leg and finishing just above ankle length. *Braces* as supports to breeches came in about 1787 and were called gallowses.

The *frock coat* was used for all undress occasions. There were many variations to the collar but, from the flat collar of the 60s, it became a high stand-fall type by the late 1780s. The curve away from the waistline with the skirts becoming narrower showed the development for the future. It was single breasted until the 1780s, without lapels, and there-

Long natural hair c 1795

Curled natural hair style c 1805

after was worn double breasted with lapels. Sleeves were loose fitting in the 1770s then became closer fitting to the wrist, cuffs with three buttons on the upper border were common in the 1760s, thereafter cuffs *à la marinière* were popular, the most popular was the vertical slit which came in fashion in the 1780s.

Outdoor wear The great coat was very large and loose reaching to just below the knees, the neck had a double or treble falling broad collar, often called capes. It fastened single breasted fashion to just below the waist. It buttoned high to the chin, lapels were uncommon, later however it became double breasted with lapels. The spencer was a short jacket with a stand-fall collar and was very popular from the 1790s onwards.

Neckwear The cravat, worn as a falling necktie, was taken up by the Macaronis and made again fashionable in the 1770s. It then had the added refinements of being made from muslin and lace edged. The solitaire was also worn at this time often with a bag wig. From 1780 the new style stock and muslin cravat, with the muslin being wound round the neck several times then secured with a knot, became the neckwear fashion.

Wigs The wearing of wigs was prevalent among all classes until the 1790s when natural hair once again became the vogue, with numerous variations. But many of them still persisted from the early part of the century. They continued to be made from human, horse hair and other such materials. A study of wigs would serve the stage historical costume designer in good stead.

Headwear The three-cornered hat remained in vogue throughout the century and altered very little from the first half of the century with few exceptions. The Macaroni hat was a rather small version usually trimmed with a feather and was placed on the top of a tall wig. The chapeau bras and the opera hat which were almost identical being cocked three-cornered hats flattened, and thus easier to carry under the arm. The bicorne, from 1780s onwards, was a hat with both the front and back brims turned up and decorated with a rosette on the left side. They came in various styles and with as many different names.

Hair brushed forward with pit-tail c 1802

Footwear continued very much on the same lines as the previous half of the century with a few modifications. Buckles went out of fashionable wear after the 1790s, being replaced by shoe strings. Many riding boot styles became walking-out boots, from about the 1780s, with such names as hessians, high-lows, Hussar buskins — and many others. Spatterdashes, and half spatterdashes, a type of gaiter were worn in the country and by soldiers.

Accessories Apart from the wearing of the sword, which became uncommon by the 1780s, the general accessories carried were similar to those in the earlier period.

Artificial aids to fashion The beaux of this period had not changed and they continued to wear rouge on their faces and lips, and to wear false calves.

Long natural hair style c 1796

Simple toupee and small side curls c 1772

Close cut style c 1810

Close curled hair c 1812

The shorter hairstyle of 1804

The French Directoire and First Empire

Following the aftermath of the Revolution a Directoire of five, with powers to act for the government of France, was formed. Nobility had returned and fashion again began to develop, this time towards the classical styles of ancient Greece and Rome. America and France had thrown off the yoke of a monarchy and now found an emotional identification with the forms and images of the ancient world. They became allies. The wars between England and France, which had begun in 1792, continued until 1804. As in all wars a great deal of creative thinking had gone into designing the military uniforms, so it was not difficult to understand that much of this rubbed off onto the fashion scene of the day.

Toupee with curls on shoulders and a queue c 1778

Men's clothes Napoleon, who gained power under the Directoire whose armies he had commanded, became Emperor of France in 1804. He provided France once again with a fashionable court, following the classical theme of the ancient Greek and Roman Empire. The Empress Josephine continued with the high waistline dresses of the last century this was followed by the Egyptian influence. Due to the Peninsular War in Spain, fashion gave way to Spanish styles, Spanish decoration being intermingled with what was thought to be a classical garment. At the end of hostilities in 1815 the English and French women's fashions had diverged with the noticeable flaring out at the hem of the French skirt. The English quickly adopted the French vogue.

Toupee with bag c 1766

Tye wig c 1778

Large bag-wig style c 1774

Pig-tail type wig c 1791

Men's coats France led the fashion in the nineteenth century as far as women's costume is concerned but not in the field of the male costume. The English 'country' clothes won the day. The general change in men's costume at the turn of the century was less dramatic than that of the women's costume. The trend towards simpler styles was a logical progression from the coats of the previous era.

Now almost universally worn in Europe and America was the frock coat, cut away at the front. There were two styles, those that were cut straight across at the waist and the others which sloped away at an angle from a high waist line. In the 1790s the single breasted wide lapel, square-cut type was the most fashionable, but by the turn of the century the double breasted version had taken over the fashionable lead.

Toupee wig style c 1790

The coat could be fastened to the neck or with the fastening of the two buttons and the top folded back to form lapels, or left unbuttoned exposing the waistcoat. The earlier coat had long tails to calf length, but now they reached only to knee level. Two pleats with buttons at the top decorated the tails. Sleeves were long to the wrist and close fitting although a little fuller at the armhole. There was no cuff, but the buttons remained as decoration. Pockets and flaps were placed at waist level on either side. These styles of tailed coats continued well into the nineteenth century, but in the first decade, the 'bob tailed' coat appeared. This was similar to the square-cut coat with the exception that the tail ends were removed, leaving a shorter tail at just below buttock length, although worn at this time it did not become fashionable wear for several decades.

Toupee with side curls c 1789

Waistcoats similar to the coats were either single or double breasted, being cut mostly across at waist level in a straight line. Sometimes however they were a little longer than the coat and could just be seen at the base of the coat. Worn with the sloping away coat the waistcoat was often cut in a double V in front. Double breasted waistcoats similar to the coat could be fastened to the neck or the top material could be folded back to form lapels, it then revealed the frilled front of the shirt, the neck being encircled with a stock and a soft material dangling bow. The waistcoats were often a different colour to the coat or they were striped.

Knee breeches continued to be worn for formal and court

Working man in a short coat with old-fashioned breeches, ticking stockings. Woollen type bonnet c 1802
Gentleman in the Court frock coat with standing collar, heavily embroidered down the front and over the pockets. Breeches and stockings c 1803

Man in frock coat cut away at the waist with long tails, narrow sleeves with puffed shoulders, rolling collar and lapels standing out from the chest and back. Waistcoat with standing stiffened lapels and high stock. Gaiter pantaloons. Beaver top hat, natural hair c 1803
Back view of the frock coat with high standing collar, exaggerated three-cornered hat c 1800

Bag-wig type c 1790

Military man in uniform with high standing collar with button and loop on either side. The coat has turned back lapels, exposing the waistcoat. The back of the tails are turned back and secured with an embroidered device. Epaulettes usually of gold or silver with fringe. White kerseymere breeches with high boots with re-enforced tops. Bicorne type hat with cockade and feather c 1799
Lady in an open front gown displaying a quilted petticoat. Shallow crowned hat of straw with a wide curved brim with a ribbon hatband. Tippet with short ends in front c 1780-1790

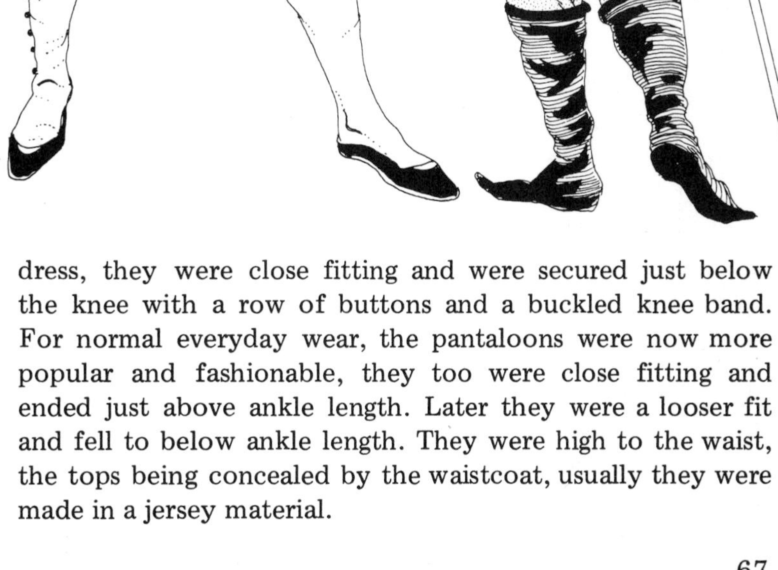

dress, they were close fitting and were secured just below the knee with a row of buttons and a buckled knee band. For normal everyday wear, the pantaloons were now more popular and fashionable, they too were close fitting and ended just above ankle length. Later they were a looser fit and fell to below ankle length. They were high to the waist, the tops being concealed by the waistcoat, usually they were made in a jersey material.

Scottish costume

In this period the traditional Scottish costume had two distinct elements — the plaid and the kilt. The only significant difference between the men's costume, and that of the women's, was the length of the kilt.

It was an Englishman by the name of Rawlinson, who worked at a foundry in the Highlands, who, in 1720, came up with the idea to cut the all-in-one plaid, which was worn at this time, into two pieces. The lower part was then wrapped round the body at the waist and fastened with a pin, this was done to allow greater movement or freedom of movement for the workmen. The upper part was then used as a scarf or plaid.

After the Jacobite rebellion of 1745 and the final defeat of the Scots at Culloden in 1746, the English Government in 1747 passed the Dress Act. This act made it illegal to 'wear or put on the clothes commonly known as Highland clothes, which is plaid, philabeg or little kilt, trowse, shoulder belt or any part whatsoever which belongs to the Highland garb; no tartan or party-coloured plaid or stuff shall be used for great coats or for upper coats'. To disobey this Act meant six months' imprisonment for the first offence and transportation to the colonies for seven years for the second, although Highland Regiments of the British Army were allowed to wear the tartan during this time. This was repealed after thirty five years.

It was not uncommon to see the chiefs of clans dressed in a jacket, trews and plaid. They wore the trews in preference to the kilt because they liked to ride horseback. The jacket in the style of the period was buttoned down the front, hip length, with a small turn-over collar. Round the neck was a stock. The trews were close-fitting breeches with the knee-bands buckled over the stockings. Over the right shoulder was a broad leather belt which supported a claymore type sword. Round the waist was a leather belt which secured the dirk dagger in the front. Over the left shoulder was slung the plaid cloak. Fashionable wigs with the bag-wig were worn in this period of 1746.

Highland soldier in kilt of the Black Watch Regiment c 1750

STAGE PROPERTIES

The term 'prop' is in common usage, it is an abbreviation of the word property, and it refers to all things in a stage production which are not under the classification of scenery or wardrobe with some few exceptions; chairs, tables are props and so are all smaller items such as drinking glasses, cups, knives, forks.

The stage designer will find it necessary to have a good property department as an integral part of the design department. Property people who can work to designs and make most of the special items required are economic common sense when working on a limited budget. But theatre properties are a complex medium and require people of many and varied talents who are able to deal with a special request and by so doing can not only preserve money but, in many cases, ensure that the production is able to have something that might otherwise have been unobtainable.

The value of a good property maker is perhaps not so much the adaptability or ability to make good props quickly and cheaply, although this is of prime importance, but in the fact that he knows the techniques and the limitations of the theatre-art crafts, and as his work is extremely varied he should be given a considerable measure of individual responsibility.

It is the stage designer's ultimate responsibility to decide how a particular property effect shall be carried out, and as there are many different ways of achieving the same result, he should work very closely with his property section, in order that they are both fully aware of all the factors involved. Special property effects must, before being included in the production, be fully evaluated.

The advent of many modern materials such as glass fibre compounds, polyester resin, latex and expanded polystyrene has improved theatre techniques considerably and the making of properties has become more and more specialized.

French Grenadier soldier dressed in the frock type coat with the turned-back and buttoned lapels. The collar was high to the chin. Short waistcoat. Breeches were worn with the high over the knee buttoned gaiters. The 'shako' headwear had a tall plume in the front. The equipment consisted of, crossbelts, backpack, bayonet, hanger sword and a musket

The girl is dressed in the nondescript clothes of a camp-follower, a laced bodice piece, skirt and apron. She wore a large straw hat worn over a mob-cap, wooden clogs c 1807

Bearing in mind these new techniques, the stage designer along with his property department, should face the production property requirements with confidence.

The *furniture* of this early Georgian period was still in the heavy Baroque style, with its massive carvings of lions' heads, masks and shells. In the town, furnishings usually of walnut wood were very fashionable but the country houses still favoured the oak, beech and elm woods.

When portraying the larger wealthier houses the stage property furniture must appear to be the rather large ostentatious type; when a middleclass set is to be visualized then the furniture is of the smaller variety.

From about the 1730s mahogany furniture became very popular and remained in vogue thereafter because of its suitability for fine carving. Popular at this time was the Chinese oriental lacquered furniture in various colours — black, red, yellow and green — this was usually the boudoir setting furniture.

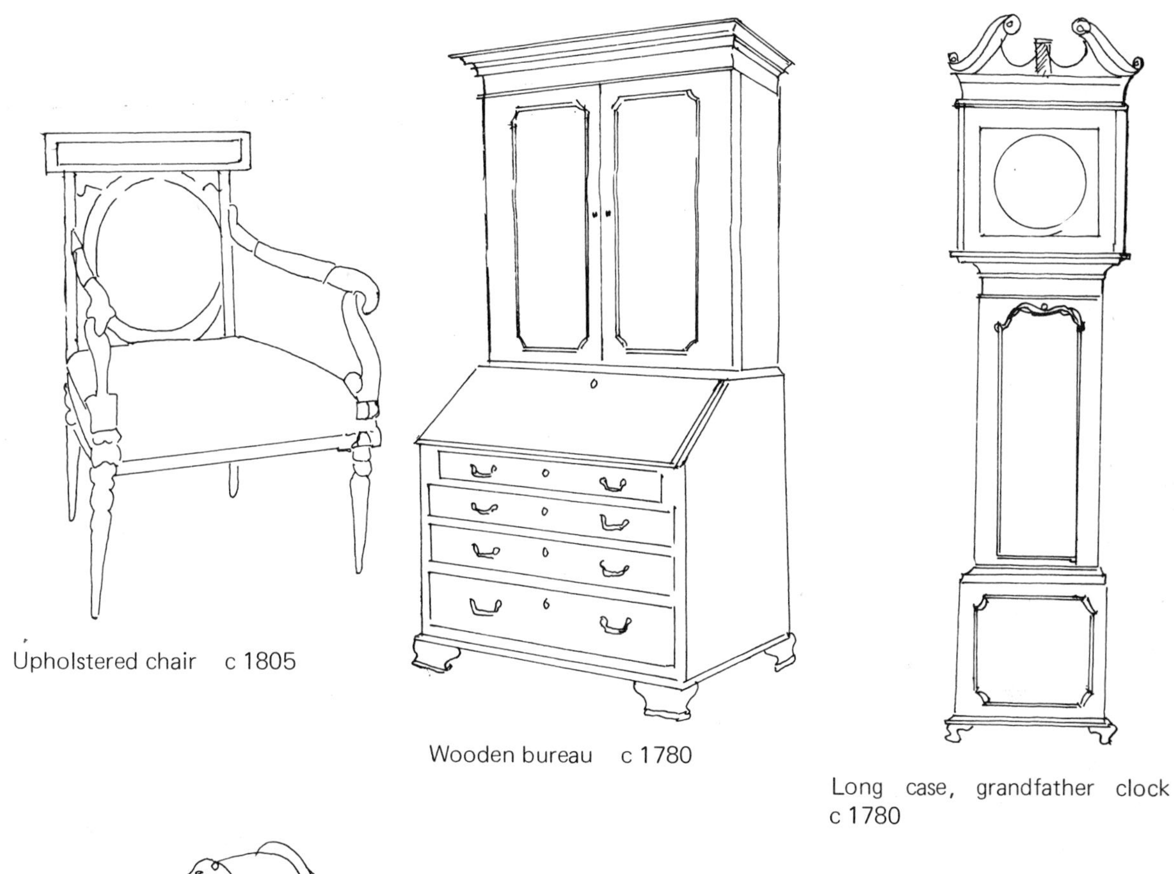

Upholstered chair c 1805

Wooden bureau c 1780

Long case, grandfather clock c 1780

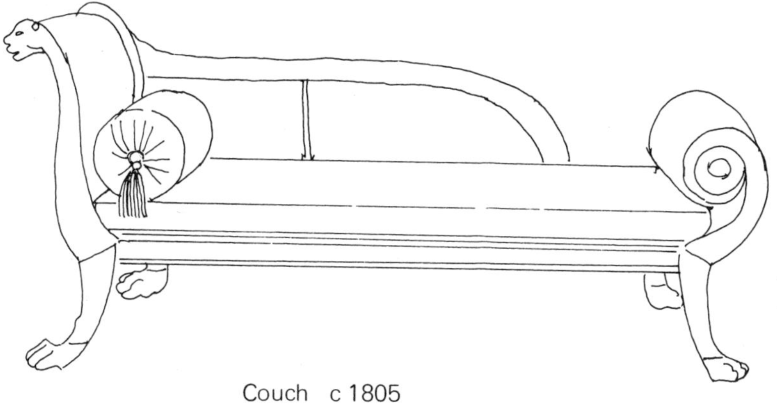

Couch c 1805

Four-poster bed design c 1745

Mahogany chair c 1750

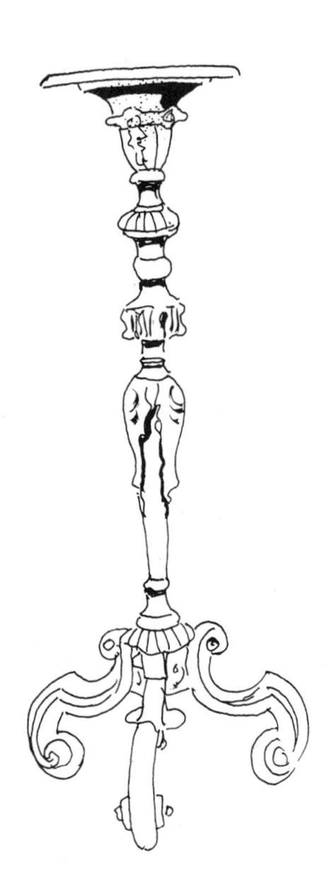

A gueridon c 1720

Settee c 1750

The lady to the left is in court dress of the period 1805, high waisted with long trained overskirt. The lady in the centre is wearing the crinoline dress used at court in the late eighteenth century. The man on the right is in an eighteenth century hunting costume, and is carrying a large hunting horn

The man on the left is in a low-neck collarless coat, and square-toed jack boots, wearing a campaign wig 1720. The lady is wearing a long polonaise crinoline style court dress of 1775. The dandy of the day is in the double breasted coat and waistcoat, full high cravat, close fitting breeches and striped stockings, 1810

A study of the architectural features of the period will show the heavy ornamentation on the larger pieces of furniture such as the enormous bedsteads and the heavy libraries and bookcases.

Styles of furnishings were named after the craftsmen of the day or the reigning monarchs, such as Louis XV, William Kent, Thomas Chippendale, and the Adam brothers. Their names followed more their style than their actual work.

Depicting a French interior the stage property furnishings must show the beginning of the more dainty, more graceful type of furniture, although still large at this period, a last lingering touch of the Baroque fashion, it was more tastefully designed in walnut or light-coloured woods, often enamelled or gilded. This type of furniture was the forerunner of the Rococo style.

The mixture of styles — Gothic, Rococo and Chinese — continued throughout the period, with them were small tables now used for the popular tea-drinking habit and the wide armed chairs specially designed for the hooped dresses of the ladies. Chairs were carved in various styles of quatrefoil shapes for the Gothic, shells for the Rococo, and filigree work with pagoda heads for the Chinese. These following the trend were painted, and upholstered in satin or tapestry. The characteristic feature of this period was the upholstery of needlepoint. This exquisite work was usually made by the ladies of the house.

The types of chairs in common use were numerous. It is sufficient to say that nearly all local museums have some of the furniture on show which is ideal for the designer's research. I will, however, mention a few of the more popular and common styles. The grandfather chair was large, winged, upholstered, often in leather, and had short Queen Anne type legs. Extremely popular and in usage in the coffee houses, public taverns and ale houses was the wheel-backed chair, this easy-to-make comfortable chair was made of a mixture of woods: elm, beech, yew or ash.

Settees usually followed the chair designs with upholstered backs and various surrounds of the period. Later they were fretted or had the Gothic style wooden backs. The upholstery was of velvet, damask or embroidery.

Tables were in various styles, the gate-leg table being the most common, usually with an oval-shaped top. The drop-leaf type was also widely used. Up to about 1740 the highly decorative marble-topped console table was very fashionable.

Later this became rather delicate in design in the Rococo style, and was usually placed against a wall. There were tables for most things; card tables, tea tables, bedside dressing tables, and work tables, all in a variety of styles of tripod or four-legged.

The early Georgian period saw a great increase in the use of mirrors, regardless of the high cost which they attracted. They were so designed and positioned to increase illumination by reflection and for their decorative value. The wooden frame surrounds were very ornate in Gothic, Chinese or French styles. Bedrooms of this era usually had dressing-glasses, which were portable type hinged small mirrors in a wooden frame. These stood on dressing-tables.

The large buffet type dresser which had been in use since the Restoration was now confined mainly to country houses, the open shelves accommodating the plates and pewter ware. The wealthier town houses were now installed with sidetables. These, however, soon changed to sideboards. Still fashionable were the storage cupboards which fitted into the corner, these had short stub type legs. Due to the great influence of the Chinese culture and art, china cabinets became increasingly fashionable. These were made either to hang or were placed on stands. They were usually glass-fronted to display the various china items. Commodes came into fashion about the middle of the century.

Libraries or bookcases were usually large heavy pieces of furniture, carved in the architectural style of the period with columns and capitals. The upper section was usually of glass, displaying the books. The lower section was cupboard space with panelled doors. Secretaries (writing desks) were more often than not massive pieces of furniture. Bureaux-cabinets were fitted with drawers with a desk top.

Still retaining its importance as the most costly item in the household in all its ornamental magnificence was the bed, massive and four-postered. The upright posts followed the trend of the architectural design with classical columns. They were high with carved tops which were concealed under a high canopy with a roof piece. To the canopy frame was attached heavy velvet, embroidered tapestry or damask draperies fringed and tasselled. Tall-boys, which were really sets of drawers placed one upon the other, dressing glasses, wash stands, shaving mirrors on a small stand support and wig stands completed the fashionable bedroom.

Clocks were an essential article of furniture and no interior stage set would be complete without this important item. There were various types from the small chimney pieces type to the large ornate grandfather clock.

Like the clock, the spinning wheel was an essential popular item of furniture and should always make its appearance somewhere on the interior set, especially when it is a middle-class home set. For exterior scenes the spinning wheel could be placed outside a worker's cottage.

The illumination of the set should be represented by chandeliers and tall carved candlestands and candelabras. These were in a variety of designs and finish, painted, gilded, or both. Hall lanterns were usually of brass frame work with glass windows.

Draught excluders, which were screens, were very necessary during this period and were positioned round the rooms at all the strategic points — in front of windows and doors to lessen the draught. These were in various designs the most fashionable and popular were the Chinese painted screens.

After the second half of the century, furniture, although basically the same, became more delicate, mainly because of the finer workmanship and design. Mahogany wood retained its popularity throughout, satin woods gained a fashionable hold along with walnut, ebony, chestnut, sycamore, rosewood and a variety of others. Chairs in the later period were characterised by their straight legs and rectangular chair backs. From about 1795 the French style of furniture became more fashionable, chairs were upholstered in silk brocade, velvet, leather or haircloth black or coloured, with their Greek or Egyptian motifs. This type of furniture can be seen for all research work in most of the museums throughout Europe and America.

The tall windows although belonging to the scenic department, are draped with curtains which are the responsibility of the property department. These were of taffeta, printed linen or damask. The draped curtains were held back by a heavy cord of gold coloured cotton and were often tasselled.

Among the many *musical instruments* which decorated the sets were the spinet, harpsichord, and lady's harp. These were usually large pieces of furniture and, if not specifically used for playing, can, with a certain amount of natural ability, be made or vamped up from odd pieces of older furniture. Those musical instruments that are carried (hand properties) by the actors or actresses should be the violin,

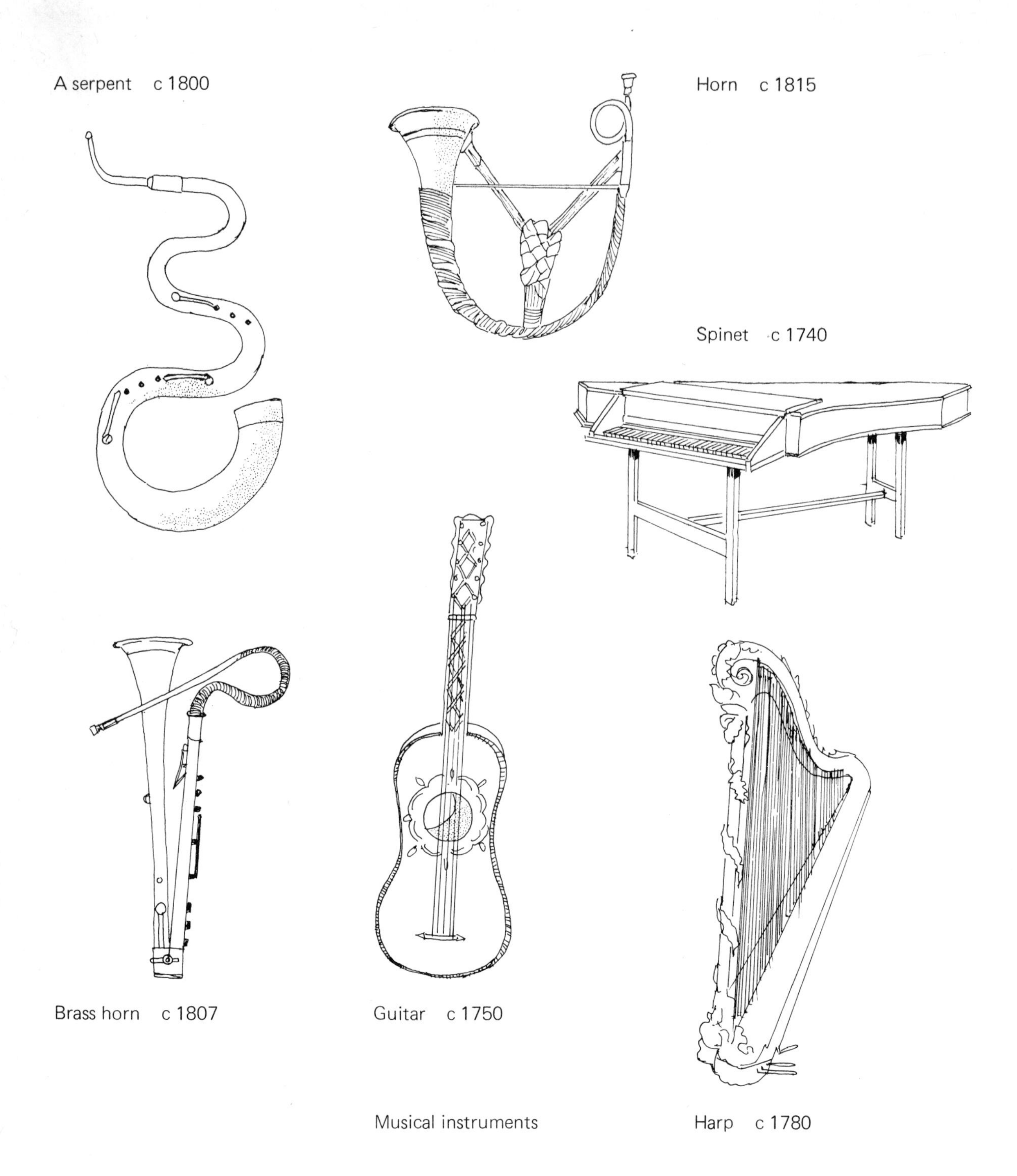

Musical instruments

guitars, flageolet and the popular transverse (a German flute). Again most musical museums have a full range of these instruments on show.

The *military weapons* for the armies of Europe were now divided into two; the gun and the sword. The gun covers the musket and the pistol and the sword the sabre and the bayonet. The continental armies had almost by this time discarded the matchlock. In Britain at the beginning of the century they had begun to develop the flintlock musket. This weapon was about 46 inches (about 1 metre 30 cm), with a longish barrel which was fitted to a walnut stock with a wooden ramrod. As the illustration shows, the stock extended almost to the end of the barrel but allowed a short length to be uncovered to permit the fixing of the bayonet. The difference between the continental French pattern musket and the British gun was the barrel fixing method: the British used the lug and pin, the French had a series of brass bands which secured both the barrel and the stock together. This basic British musket became known as the Brown Bess and remained in service with the army for over one hundred years. A smaller version was carried by the cavalry and known as a carbine. During the eighteenth century there were numerous types of guns both for the military and for civilian use, for the latter these were hunting guns or the coaching 'blunderbuss' used as protection by the guards of the Royal Mail Coaches. The military by the eighteenth century were carrying the cartridge bag and slowly discarding the powder flask. It was the reverse with the sportsman, he still preferred the flask in one form or the other. The military pistol was again more of a practical weapon and was very plain and lacking in decoration, unlike their continental counterpart whose flintlock pistols tended to be more decorative. Civilian pistols were the duelling pistols and the pocket defensive small pistol.

Every gentleman wore a small sword although this was gradually being discarded during the eighteenth century and finally about 1780 was generally abandoned. These swords had a variety of hilts and scabbards too numerous to list here, so therefore I do recommend a study of one of the many sword books which are on the market or a further visit to your local Military museum where you will find many of these, and all the military swords at the same time. The usual military sword was often much heavier and longer than the civilian type. Bayonets were not attached to the muskets by using a tubular socket which fitted over the muzzle end and secured in position by a stud.

When the main body armour was finally discarded a large

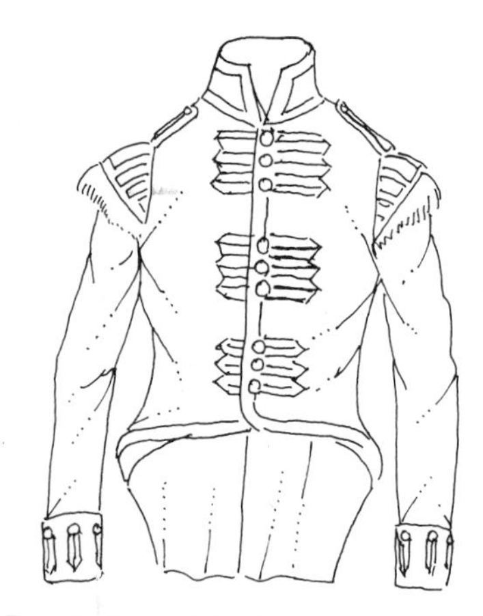
Front view of tunic

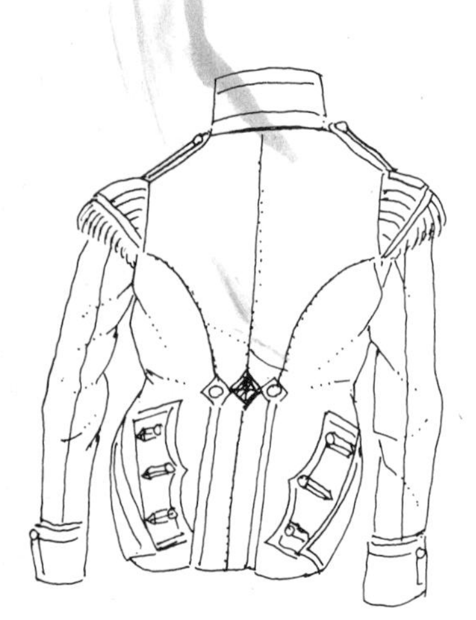
Back view of tunic

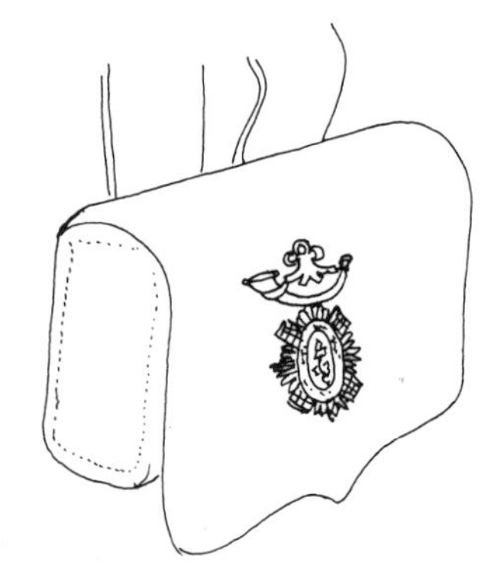
Black leather ammunition pouch

Soldier in full battle kit

British soldier of 1815

Waterloo shako

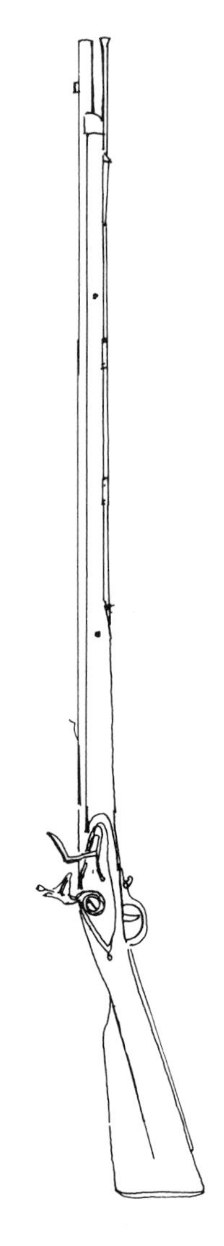
Brown Bess musket

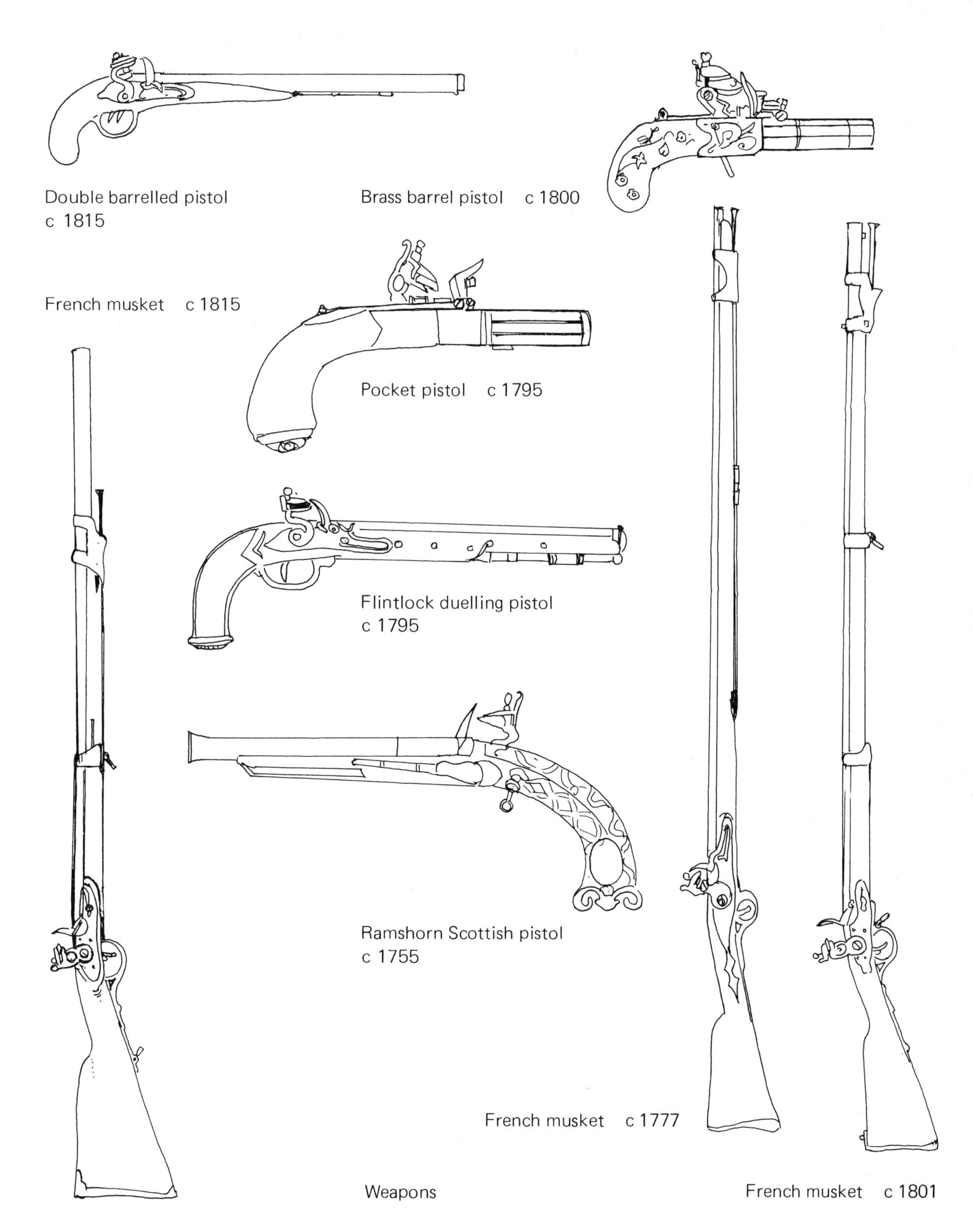

Double barrelled pistol c 1815

Brass barrel pistol c 1800

French musket c 1815

Pocket pistol c 1795

Flintlock duelling pistol c 1795

Ramshorn Scottish pistol c 1755

French musket c 1777

Weapons

French musket c 1801

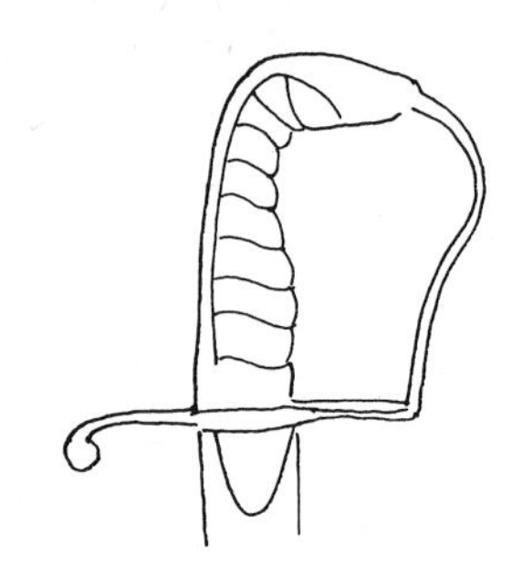

Stirrup hilt c 1796

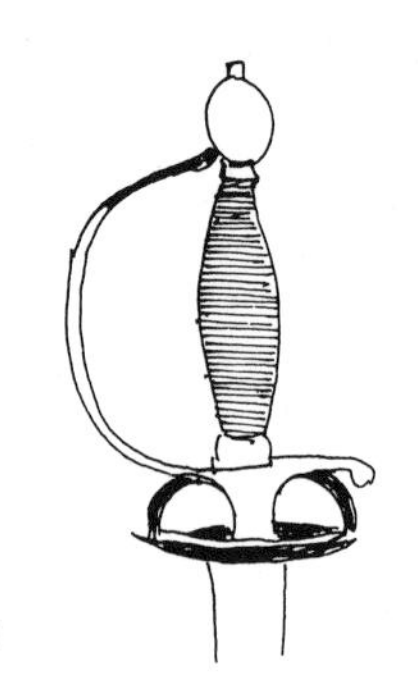

c 1760

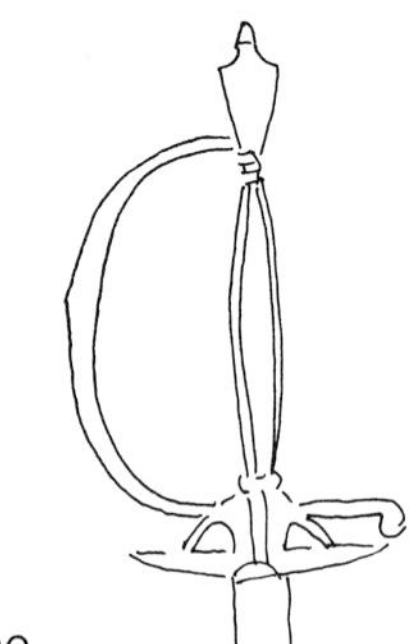

c 1790

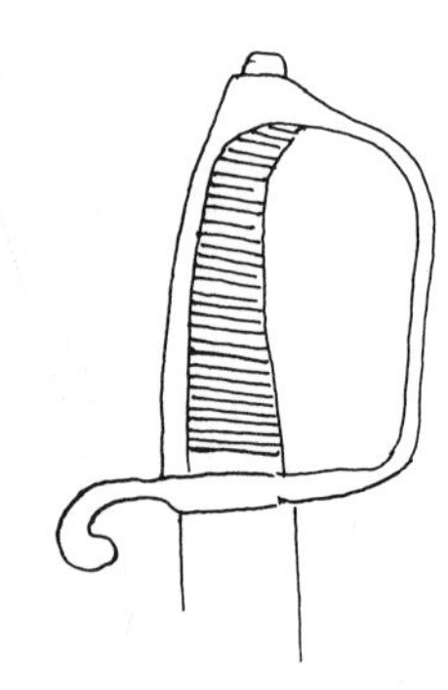

Hanger sword c 1815

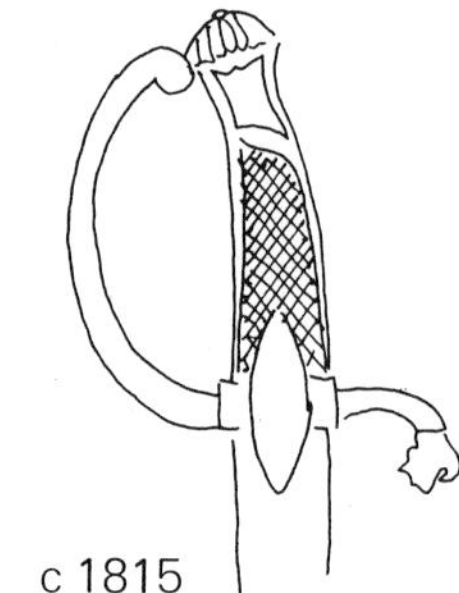

Sabre c 1815

Scottish claymore c 1778

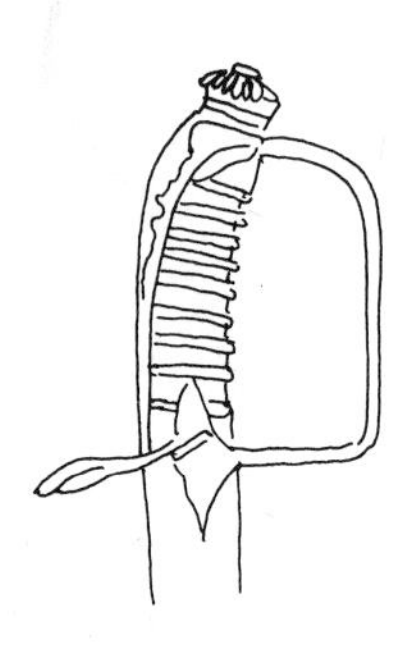

Guards pattern sword c 1815

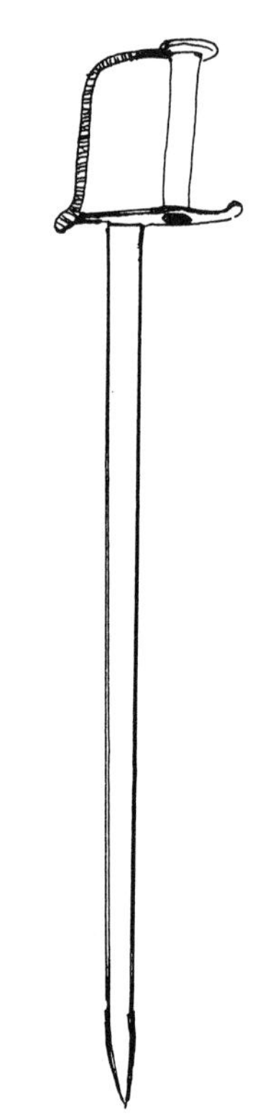

Sword bayonet c 1800

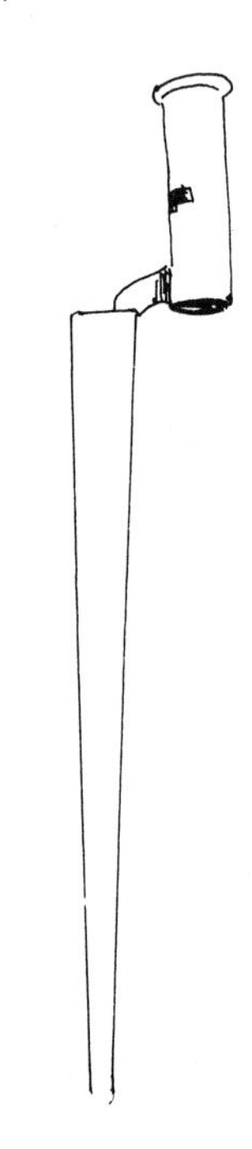

Bayonet c 1720

crescent-shaped piece of metal was hung around the neck, which was purely symbolic of a past age. During the eighteenth century these became smaller and in 1796 it was decreed that these gorgets as they were called should bear the royal cipher and wreath. This item was worn by officers as a distinction of rank and sometimes by the senior non-commissioned officers.

The lance which had been out of service for many years, in England since the civil war, was again brought back, this time by Napoleon for his famous Polish Guards. This set again the fashion for cavalry to carry this weapon, the British followed on and equipped her cavalry with the lance and pennant.

Standard equipment for the soldiers of this period for the cavalry was: the sword belt, sword knot, slings and bayonet frog, pouch and carbine belt and a black leather cartridge pouch. This was fairly standard for all British and continental troopers. The infantry also carried very much the same type of equipment: cross belt with bayonet frog, cartridge pouch, bread bag, back pack equipment. Naturally they differed to some degree but a glance through some of the many books on military uniform will show what is required.

Kitchen utensils followed the earlier period being made from wood, pewter, brass, iron, earthenware and glass. Warming pans of various sizes were very popular and most necessary — these were made of brass or copper. If a kitchen scene is to be staged do not forget the brick circular oven usually at the side of the fire; this was closed with an iron door. Also a turning spit was still in use for the larger joints of meat. The usual articles — pots of various shapes and sizes, skillets, frying pans, pans, barrels, tubs, ladles — were still in use.

This was a period of beautiful china and glassware, and the wealthier households were decorated with silverware created by the Huguenot silversmiths who had fled earlier from France. Rococo ornamentation was apparent at this time and could be seen in the new vogue of tea drinking in the teapots, tea caddies, tea kettles, jugs, trays and spoons. Other articles included large and small candlesticks, chocolate pots, inkstands and many other objects. Later porcelain products took over many of the functions of the silverware, for the set-designers concern this change-over took place about the 1750s.

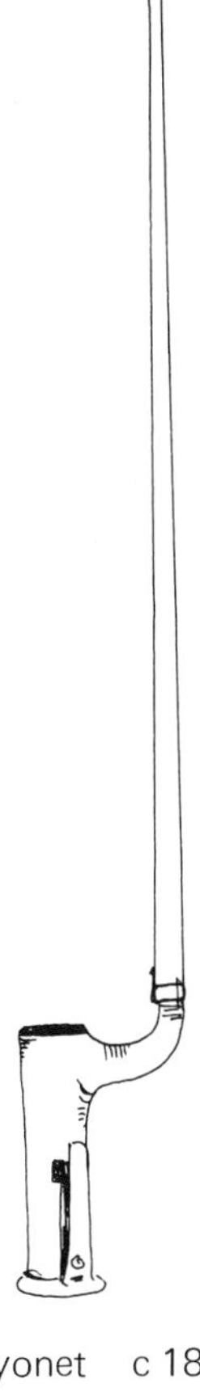

Socket bayonet c 1800

Tankard c 1720

Drinking tankard c 1750

Drinking mug c 1720

Tea caddy c 1758

Tea kettle c 1730

Chocolate pot c 1722

Wine bottle c 1710

Silver teapot c 1790

Hand properties These are props which although are an essential part of costume come under the property department's responsibility. Costume jewellery and accessories come under this heading. The fashionable men up to 1780, or thereabouts, always carried a short sword and also affected a long, silver headed malacca cane (although short canes were also carried). The beaux at this time always carried a cane and made a great business of strutting about with one usually with elegant carved heads. Heavier sticks of oak or cudgel sticks were often carried by the ordinary people or by workers, this fashion was sometimes copied by the fashionable young bucks. Umbrellas for men did not become fashionable until the middle of the century, even then it was considered effeminate to carry one. Fans were only carried by the fops and dandies of the period. Jewellery for men was used somewhat sparingly, this being confined to mainly ornate shoe, knee and stock buckles. Watches, however, were popular and came in decorative cases or on short ribbon or goldstrands; seals also were allowed to dangle from the fob pocket of the breeches. Two watches became fashionable wear from the 1770s until the 1780s then it became fashion again to wear just one. Snuff boxes were popular and carried by nearly all men of fashion, these were in small boxes made from silver, gilt or ivory. The fan was universally popular and essential for all fashionable ladies, they came in various sizes but most popular was the folding variety. Face masks both full and half sizes were in use until the 1760s. Both canes and umbrellas were carried by women. Jewellery was not profusely worn and was mainly pearl necklaces, earrings, lockets, crosses, jewelled buckles on shoes and girdles. Similar to the male fashion was the wearing of watches one either side during this fashionable fad. Bosom bottles to contain flowers (real or artificial) were attached to the dress. Towards the end of the century in the 1790s the carrying of handbags came into fashion, these were called ridicules or indispensibles.

The making of properties is always a problem, whether it is more advisable to hire many of the articles remains the unanswerable question. In my opinion it is better to try and produce as many of the articles oneself as in the long run mounting costs can certainly curtail any ambitious ideas the smaller production companies may wish to entertain. Remember it is not required for a stage production to have a fine detailed finish, the main shape and outline are all that is required. Try the various materials which are now available on the market, some are very good and will I feel sure fulfil their purpose.

STAGE SETTINGS

The art of stage set designing is quite different from other art forms, if anything it is a combination of the artist and the architect. It is a never-ending ranging of creative impulses and expressions which, because of their variations and nature, need great research and study. The prime factor is to remember that the set when completed will have all the atmosphere and feeling of the suggested period and yet will still only be a part of the whole production. A set which 'up stages' both costume and actor is bad scenic design, and has not fulfilled its true purpose. Therefore, from the outset, there must be a perfect co-ordination between the four main sections: scenic, costume, lighting and the actors.

The method of approach is entirely the wish of the designer, subject of course, to the consent of the production team, whether it be realistic, symbolic or in an expressionistic vein. Whichever way, it must express the correct atmosphere and character of that historical period of the play and the basic architectural forms should be incorporated.

The all-important feature that the designer must bear in mind is that the set must conform in every way to the requirements of the action of the play. This needs careful planning and discussion to create the right grounding for the idea. It is essential to read the play and to grasp the meaning of the author's conception, and intention.

A good designer must have the ability and the dramatic and imaginative impulse to transfer his basic sketch from the drawing board to an ambitiously built stage picture. Also to be able to study and comprehend all the salient arts that go into making a production of an historical play, and to have a clear and comprehensive understanding of the principles of modern stagecraft. Without all these things, which must be coupled with ingenuity and invention, the design will lack that flourish of inspiration which makes a living scene.

Cut-out gate piers, can be used also as a centre piece with or without gates. Set against a cyclorama

Typical doorway with rusticated ionic columns centre piece. If used as a practical door it will require a backing piece

Architecture plays a great part in the planning of an historical stage set, so a study of the houses and buildings of that period is most essential. In this volume we are dealing with the Late Renaissance, which was an era roughly from about the beginning of the eighteenth century and continuing through to the nineteenth century.

The main character of the Renaissance architecture depended very much on the whims and fancies of the architects of the day. What was important was the standardisation of the domestic architecture that achieved the feeling of restfulness both in design and appointments. The great demand for houses for the middle classes, and the larger mansion type for the wealthier, had brought about this feeling in the new designs.

There is of necessity a great overlapping between volumes three and four in regard to architectural constructions as one ended and the other began in the era of the Late Renaissance. In the one we have the planning and the erecting of these buildings and the other of the continuance and occupation. Both paying their lip service to this period of the eighteenth century.

Ornamental wall mirror can be hung on a suitable painted flat to convey the period

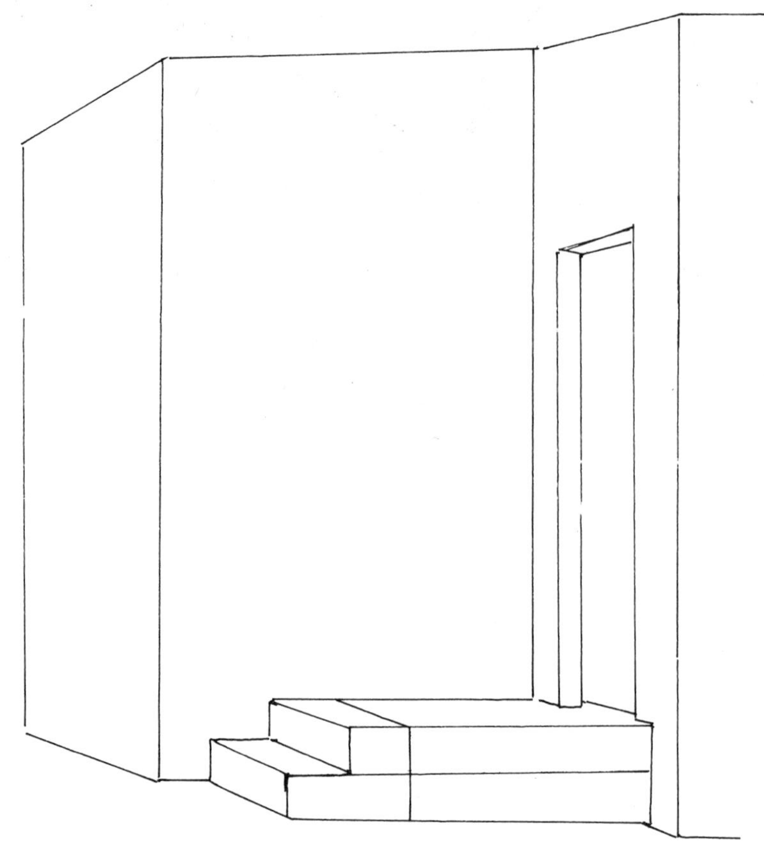

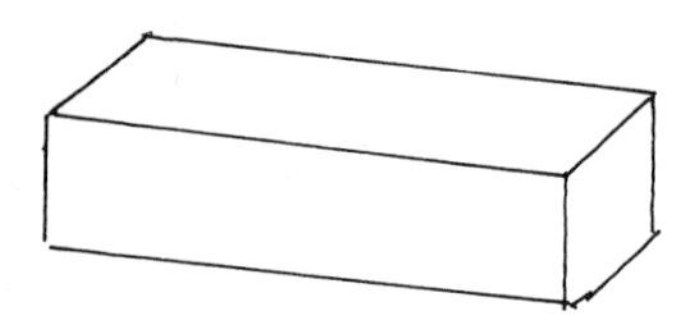

Single step piece

Straight flats set-up, door opening, rostrum and steps

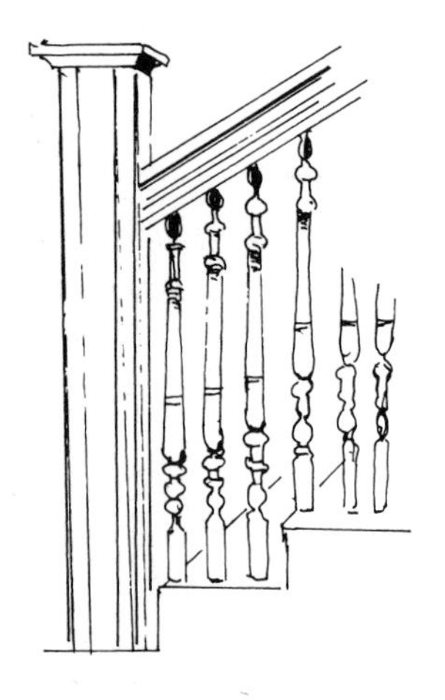

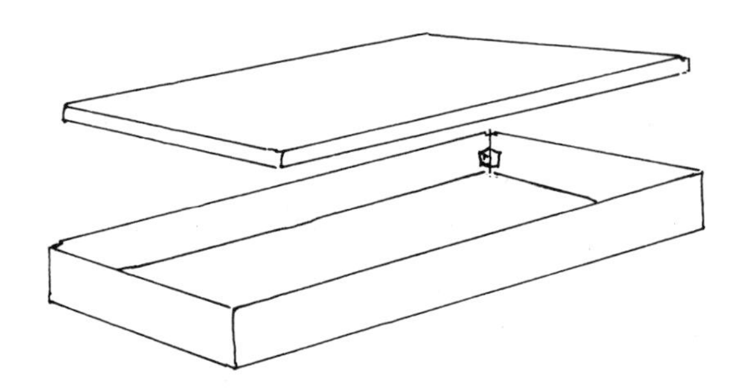

Rostrum frame and top to fit

Type of handrails of the period

Architecture had now taken on a regularity and often exaggerated symmetry, which brought about a unification of the many facets into an effective facade. The walls sometimes ended with impressive cornices in brick, stone or wood which, when painted with matching colour of the window frames, gave an agreeable feature to the facade, especially when they were of red brick. The walls were of stone often simulated by stucco and, as mentioned above, were also made in brickwork.

A familiar feature of this period was the arcades, which were formed of columns constructed in the correct classical proportions. Those with superimposed orders became systematised. Doorways now became more formal in design. The classical line was to be seen even in the mouldings and, whether in stone, wood, or plaster were increasingly bolder, and those around the panels and fireplaces were larger, in the 'ogee' form. Ornamentation had lost all trace of the Gothic influence and developed into the Italian Renaissance classical tradition. The style of Louis XIV affected the whole

Door flat, painted in the style of the period

Chimney piece, this can be painted or built if required for a practical use

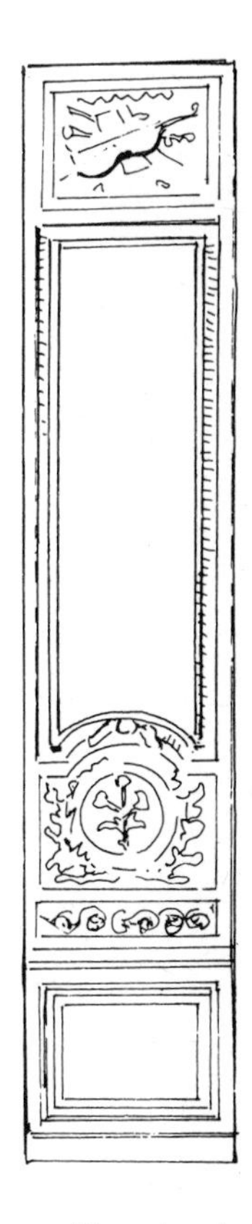

Sample of the panelling in the period

Exterior scene, built with three entrances, left, right and centre

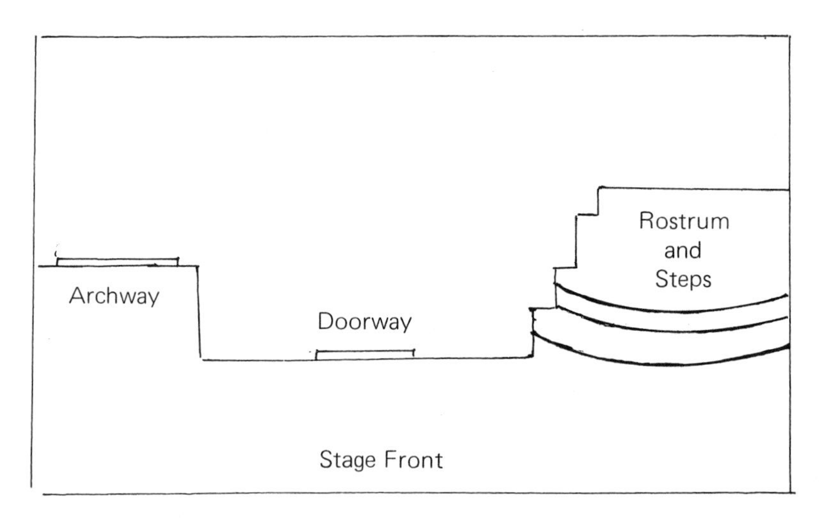

Simple stage plan of the above set

of Europe including England where the English designers took up the simpler classical traditions in their designs.

House interiors showed a greater variety in the decoration. The classical tradition was uppermost in selection, although walls continued to be of wood panelling in pinewood, and later in mahogany and carved in the classical ornamentation, they began to be covered in other ways. Stucco-decorated walls in the classical form with plaster embellishment became fashionable. This latest design included scrolls, shells, birds and ribbons in elegant compositions. In the first half of the century the woodwork was enamelled in white or cream and the wall spaces were filled with brocaded silk, tapestry or painted panels. The Chinese influence was very popular and many designs included Chinese scenes, incorporated in the interior decoration, copied from Chinese sources. From about 1750 the alternative wall covering was introduced — that of wallpaper. This at first was mainly imported from the East, again chiefly Chinese designs, but later in the century printed patterned wallpaper became very fashionable and popular. At first in a monochrome of classical sculptured figures; later printed in various colours depicting floral or landscape designs. Due to the high cost of wallpapers they were not stuck on to the walls but on to canvas screens stretched onto wooden frames then attached to the walls by means of wooden pegs. Many samples of these can be seen in museums in a well-preserved state.

A general description of the interiors may be of some help to the stage designer although this must in no way detract from the serious business of personal research.

In the first half of the century for interiors it was usual to have panelled walls of pinewood, painted either white or cream, the general woodwork such as door frames, doors and window surrounds were of the same colour. Sometimes the panelled walls were painted in an olive green. The mouldings were carved and gilded. About mid-century the painted stucco walls with gilded decoration were very fashionable. Wallpaper was now in vogue and covered the wall down to the wainscot level depicting Chinese style murals. For bedrooms at this period walls were often covered with silk draperies also down to wainscot level. After the second half of the century interiors began to be painted in different pastel shades for the background and white stucco decoration. The kitchens at this time could well be represented with wooden ceilings of beams and rafters, and plastered stone walls. The oven with the iron door is at the side of the fireplace. There was usually a stone sink with cupboard space below.

The stage properties are in their own section, but it must be remembered that they must in the first instance be incorporated in the design of the stage set designer. It is the responsibility of the set designer to signify the correct piece of furniture and its place on the set.

Further study of this period is essential if the designer is to make the historical play come to life. If the set and the properties are artistically authentic the audience will accept lack of fine detail but woe betide the designer who takes short cuts and fills his set misleadingly; audiences seem to know instinctively and the whole production could be spoilt.

Whether dealing with costume or stage settings, it cannot be over emphasized that the general silhouette is the most important feature to drive to attain, especially in historical plays.

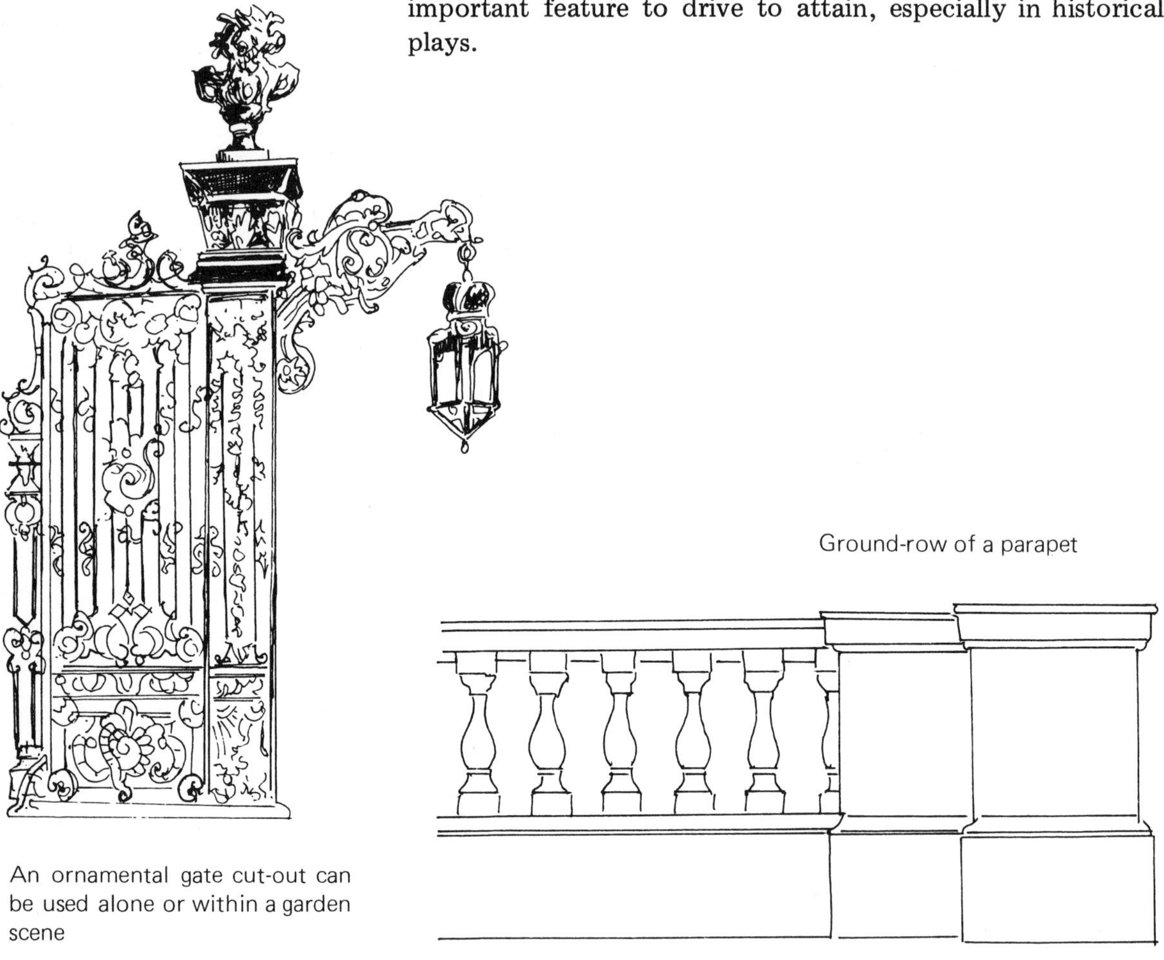

Ground-row of a parapet

An ornamental gate cut-out can be used alone or within a garden scene

STAGE LIGHTING

Lighting today is such an integral part of stage presentation, that it is very difficult to separate it from all the other facets of stage design, it is, by its very nature, a subject that allows considerable scope for individual ingenuity.

Shape and movement are the heart beat of the theatre, and, since illumination determines the ultimate appearance of shape, it is necessary to assume that stage lighting should be planned alongside of scenic and costume designs with considerable care so that it plays an unquestionable and deliberate role in the final stage picture.

Stage lighting is an art and, as such, must be treated with the same care and attention as all the other theatre arts. The stage designer, to have a sense of unity for the production, must know everything that is involved to create the whole. He must, therefore, school himself in all the arts that are working for the final dramatic effect of the play. The technique of stage lighting must be part of the stage designers 'make up', it is both a science and an art. He must begin to learn how to use light and colour effectively to build up artistic creative lighting that is pleasing, dramatically imaginative, and has an emotional appeal.

It is important to make lighting an interesting feature of the stage production, so it is essential that it should be considered in the early planning days and not at a later stage in the production budget after the sets and costumes have been made. Even the movement of the actor must take its place in the planning, if the lighting is to fulfil its proper function in the overall stage picture. No final decision of colour and materials should be finalized before the lighting has been discussed.

The combination of light and colour should be based on intelligent, imaginative thinking. With this firmly in mind it will not be too difficult to arrange good lighting constructions.

In many historical plays it is usual to arrange and stage the production so that costume, scenery and lighting give an appearance of realism. With costume especially, if made a little more colourful than normal, the larger than life effect will respond very effectively to changes in the colour of the illumination. With the correct lighting the production becomes more interesting and more colourful whilst still retaining an effect of realism and becomes more picturesque and pleasing to the eye of the audience.

Scenic and costume design are not, however, confined to any one type of lighting; they offer great opportunities for individualism and discretion. Lighting can express in a symbolic or expressionist way effects rather than realism. Three-dimensional set pieces with rostrum and steps, painted white or in a light pastel colour can be made into a scene of unusual beauty by the use of contrived and thoughtfully planned lighting with contrasting colours. This effect can be further improved by displaying the sets against a cyclorama background which, in turn, is also lit with coloured lighting.

Stage lighting is a vast subject that can be discussed at great length, but it is sufficient for me to say to the would-be stage designer, study carefully this aspect of stage theatre craft: this will facilitate and further the improvement of the production, the extent of the improvement being decided only by the type of equipment available.

Stage lighting is expensive, but, today, designers depend more and more on light to give them many of the effects so important to the dramatic and atmospheric background they need.

CHOOSING A PLAY

The historical play not only possesses the power to entertain the public it also has the ability to educate. The 'live' theatre is a real living thing, it has its own ideals, individual thoughts, feelings, peculiar practices and an external material expression all its very own, yet closely related to all that has gone before, and totally inseparable from our modern way of life.

Contemporary historical plays appeal to the imagination as they carry the audience away from the commonplace life of today into the world of yesteryear, showing the ideals and ideas which prevailed at that period. People are interested in the thinking of those times, it was the forecast of the world today and contributed to the formation of our present civilization.

Choosing a play is largely a matter of finance, ability available, time and limitation of stage and equipment. Anything which limits the producer's freedom of movement is always unpopular. The selection of historical plays of this period is certainly plentiful with something to suit all drama societies, large and small. The play-reading will determine to what extent the production can take on scenically, costume wise, lighting and in space acting area.

Historical play catalogues from the best bookshops will guide you along the right lines as to the type of stage settings, costumes and, most important, the number of people required to act out the play. The choice is fairly large but with plays from such dramatic writers as Shaw, Sheridan and Thackeray, it will be difficult to go wrong. You will be in good company working with the words of some of the greatest dramatists the world has known.

As a guide to the period of this volume I have compiled a list of plays which have, over the years, been performed by professional companies, amateur stage societies, drama groups and schools.

Here is a selection of popular plays of this period

Richard Brinsley Sheridan
School for Scandal
The Rivals
The Duenna

Oliver Goldsmith
She Stoops to Conquer

J.L. Balderston
Berkeley Square

George Farquhar
Recruiting Officer
Beaux' Stratagem

John Gay
Beggar's Opera
Polly

George Lillo
The London Merchant
(edited by
William H McBurney)

Tom Robertson
David Garrick

Langdon Mitchell
Becky Sharp
(dramatisation of
Thackeray's *Vanity Fair*)

Louise M Parker
Pomander Walk

George Bernard Shaw
The Man of Destiny

James Barrie
Quality Street

Jane Austen
Pride and Prejudice

Gullivers Travels by Jonathan Swift and *Robinson Crusoe* by Daniel Defoe are re-enacted in various ways in English pantomimes usually staged in the period costume. These and others are available in play form.

INDEX